BRING THE OUTSIDE IN

SANTA & COLE
Design Editions | Ediciones de diseño

ABI DARE

PHOTOGRAPHY BY
TIFF GRANT-RILEY

BRING THE OUTSIDE IN

BIOPHILIC DESIGN FOR A NATURALLY BEAUTIFUL HOME

RYLAND PETERS & SMALL

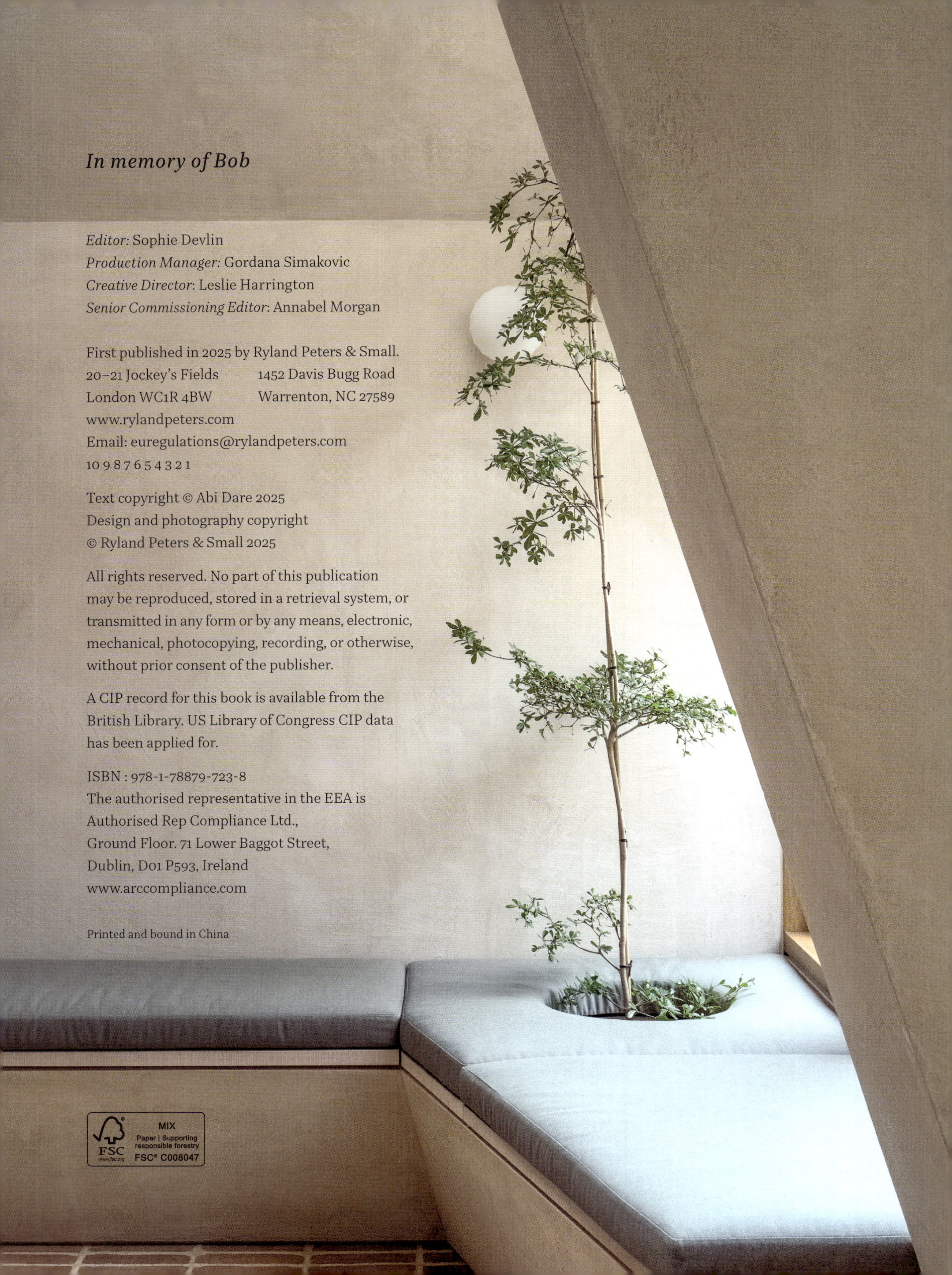

In memory of Bob

Editor: Sophie Devlin
Production Manager: Gordana Simakovic
Creative Director: Leslie Harrington
Senior Commissioning Editor: Annabel Morgan

First published in 2025 by Ryland Peters & Small.
20–21 Jockey's Fields
London WC1R 4BW
1452 Davis Bugg Road
Warrenton, NC 27589
www.rylandpeters.com
Email: euregulations@rylandpeters.com
10 9 8 7 6 5 4 3 2 1

A CIP record for this book is available from the British Library. US Library of Congress CIP data has been applied for.

ISBN : 978-1-78879-723-8
The authorised representative in the EEA is
Authorised Rep Compliance Ltd.,
Ground Floor. 71 Lower Baggot Street,
Dublin, D01 P593, Ireland
www.arccompliance.com

Printed and bound in China

CONTENTS

INTRODUCTION

CALL OF THE WILD

Despite the increasingly urban and indoor nature of 21st-century life, we remain biologically hard-wired to feel the pull of nature. Biophilic design responds to this, boosting our physical and psychological wellbeing by reconnecting us to the natural world through architecture and interiors (*opposite and above*). Its results are proven – and, despite common assumptions, plants are only one part of the picture.

Have you ever noticed how a woodland walk can make daily stresses melt away? How the solution to a tricky work problem often pops into your head during a lunchtime breather in the local park? Or how taking your morning coffee out to the garden sets you up for a brighter and more productive day? That's because we humans have an innate desire to connect with nature. We have an affinity for it, we feel better when we're surrounded by it, and despite all the technology available to us today, we're still largely dependent on it. Put simply, nature isn't just a 'nice to have', but essential to our wellbeing.

Biophilic design taps into this need by incorporating links to the natural world into the built environment – something that's more vital than ever before, as most of us now spend the majority of our time indoors. Its benefits on our mental and physical health are proven, with numerous studies revealing that bringing the outdoors in can reduce anxiety, lower blood pressure and improve our focus, energy levels and creativity. Some research has even suggested that it encourages healing after illness – a 1984 project by Roger S. Ulrich of Sweden's Chalmers University of Technology, for example, indicated that hospital patients recover sooner from surgery if they have a view of vegetation or water.

Many people mistakenly assume that biophilic design simply means filling a room with plants, but it encompasses much more than that. It's about responding to our deep-rooted emotional and sensory needs by combining direct and indirect references to the natural world through things such as colour, texture and light – and it's something we can all introduce into our homes, no matter what our budget or where we live.

Over the next 200 pages, I'll guide you through the key elements of biophilic design, explaining the psychology behind them in an easy-to-digest manner and providing clear, practical advice that you can apply yourself. I'll also take you inside 12 real-life homes across the UK and Europe that demonstrate biophilic design in action in a wide range of spaces and settings, from small city apartments to spacious country houses.

My hope is that this book will give you the tools and inspiration you need to start harnessing the power of biophilic design to create a happy, healthy and naturally beautiful home – whether you're embarking on a full renovation or self-build project, redecorating a single room or merely looking to make a few small changes that will have a big impact.

A BRIEF HISTORY OF BIOPHILIC DESIGN

The word 'biophilia' comes from the Greek for 'love of life and living things'. It was first coined by American psychoanalyst Erich Fromm in 1964 and popularized two decades later by biologist Edward O. Wilson, who argued in his 1984 book of the same name that we all yearn for nature.

The concept of biophilic design emerged in the early 2000s, when Stephen R. Kellert of Yale University published a series of books and papers focusing on the advantages of including natural references in architecture, urban planning and interiors. The idea was nothing new; in fact humans had been designing in this way for millennia. The ancient Chinese created indoor lotus pools, the Romans painted murals depicting trees and lakes, and pioneering 19th-century nurse Florence Nightingale introduced larger windows into hospitals so that patients could benefit from the healing influence of daylight. Nevertheless, it was the first time it had been given a specific name and explored in depth.

Since then, biophilic design has developed into a multifaceted and much-researched field, with specialist strands relating to homes, healthcare settings and the workplace. But you don't need to be a scientist or a design professional to start creating spaces that nurture you through nature, as this book will demonstrate.

UNIVERSAL APPEAL

Biophilic design isn't a fleeting trend, and humans have been using nature as a source of inspiration for as long as we've been constructing buildings. It isn't restricted to a particular style of decor or to a particular setting, either – it's a holistic approach that can be applied to any type of home, from minimalist urban abodes to rustic country cottages and historical houses (*this page and opposite*).

WHITE
CLASSIQUES
HOME
THE KINFOLK HOME

THE BIOPHILIC PRINCIPLES

Many biophilic design experts speak of three main principles:

- 'Nature in the space' focuses on creating a direct experience of nature by introducing elements such as plants, water, fresh air, light and sounds.

- 'Natural analogues' refers to mimicking aspects of nature through indirect means like colour, materials, artworks and shape.

- 'Nature of the space' centres around spatial configurations that evoke the natural settings and landscapes we're instinctively drawn towards.

Rather than address each of these pillars in turn, I've chosen to explore them through six sections that cover the core aspects of home decorating: colour, materials and texture, shape and pattern, light, layout and view, and finishing touches. My aim throughout is to demonstrate that biophilic design isn't a complicated or abstract theory – it's an accessible concept that can make a noticeable difference to our homes and everyday lives.

BACK TO NATURE

There are many different ways to incorporate nature into the home (*opposite and this page*). Some are instantly noticeable, for example maximizing natural light, adding flowers and foliage or showcasing views of landscapes, trees and gardens. Others, such as using artworks, shapes, colours and layouts that reference various aspects of the natural world, are much more subtle, but their impact is no less powerful.

COLOUR PALETTES

Colour is the most immediately obvious element of decor and it has a big impact on how a space looks and feels. It's also one of the easiest ways to incorporate natural elements into your home.

Nature provides endless inspiration for colours and combinations, from neutral to bold. Take the mood you want to create in any given room as a starting point and think of the hues of outdoor settings that evoke similar feelings. There's no right or wrong answer, given that our reaction to colour is a deeply personal matter shaped by individual experiences and memories – the key is finding a palette that resonates with you.

Once you have your colours in mind, test them out in situ before committing, as varying light causes the same hues to look very different in different settings. In the northern hemisphere, north-facing spaces generally receive cool light that makes colours appear colder; south-facing ones get more golden light that makes them seem warmer. The light in east- and west-facing spaces, meanwhile, changes from warm in the morning to cool in the afternoon and vice versa. In the southern hemisphere, the reverse is true.

PLANTS AND TREES

The green of vegetation often springs straight to mind when we think of nature, and we tend to find it very calming (*opposite and above right*). Some studies have suggested that our hunter-gatherer origins mean we instinctively link it with security and abundance; others that we find it less straining than other hues because it sits at the centre of the visible light spectrum and can be detected more easily.

Natural greens run the full scale from fresh mints to dark forest tones. If you want a particularly soothing option, try sage, which is tempered with grey. For something warmer, try greens with yellow undertones such as olive and apple.

Of course, greens aren't the only colours associated with plants and trees. Flowers and berries come in almost any hue, while autumn foliage can inspire schemes based around reds and oranges. Some people find these colours energizing, but for others they're overwhelming. To tone them down, look for blackened or brown-tinged shades such as burgundy and russet, or use them as an accent only.

WATER AND SKY

Many of us associate water and the sky with peace and relaxation, so blue often has the same connotations (*left*). Pale, grey-based blues can be especially restful, possibly because they're so prevalent in the natural world that they have an easy familiarity. They can also lend a wonderful airiness to a space.

If you like the tranquillity of blue but find it cold, use a greenish blue with a dash of yellow. Or, for something with a touch of drama, try the indigo of a deep, inky pool. There are plenty of vibrant blues for lovers of strong colour, too – just think of the azure of a tropical sea. And remember that water and sky are not always blue. Sunset, for example, brings a blaze of pinks, oranges and purples.

EARTH, SAND AND STONE

Also widespread across the natural world are the browns, beiges and greys of earth, sand and stone (*below*). They can form the basis of grounding neutral schemes, from pale tones reminiscent of pebbles and rocks to darker shades that evoke clay and soil. For a richer alternative, look for red- and yellow-based options such as terracotta, adobe pink, ochre and umber (*below left*).

BLACK AND WHITE

Black and white are found throughout nature – in marble, feathers, clouds and shells – and offer a simple way to introduce contrast to a biophilic scheme (*above*). Black accents can add depth and structure; white elements can lift a room, providing a dose of freshness that makes everything else sing. A word of caution, though: pure, brilliant white rarely appears in the natural world and can look stark and artificial. For a more harmonious effect, try a softer off-white instead.

BUILDING A PALETTE

There are three main approaches when it comes to combining colours. Tonal schemes mix lighter and darker versions of the same base hue for an elegant, layered look. Analogous schemes create more impact by bringing together colours that sit next to each other on the colour wheel, while complementary schemes go one step further and pair colours on opposite sides of the wheel. Keep in mind that painting the walls isn't the only way to bring in colour – ceilings, woodwork/trim, flooring, furniture and accessories should also be considered as part of your palette (*below*). If you're struggling, then picture those natural settings once again, as groupings found in nature are likely to work in the home, too. For example, the various greens of a woodland canopy form a tonal scheme, the pinks and oranges of a sunset an analogous scheme and the yellow sand and blue sky of a beach a complementary one.

EARTHY NEUTRALS

'Natural, warm and calming' is how Kine Ask Stenersen and Kristoffer Eng, founders of kitchen, furniture and interior-design studio Ask og Eng, describe their Norwegian home. Located in the port city of Drammen, to the south-west of Oslo, it's decorated in a soothing blend of muted hues inspired by earth, wood and stone, with pared-back furniture and lots of texture.

Constructed in 1868 for the director of the nearby railway station, the house once sat on a substantial plot. This had largely been eaten up by neighbouring developments by 2020, when Kine and Kristoffer moved in with their two sons Vilmer and Artur, now aged 10 and six, but the building itself had lost none of its character – something that the couple, who both grew up in Drammen, were keen to preserve. 'We'd wanted an old brick house like this for a long time,' says Kine. 'We were captivated by its charm, so our aim was to respect its history while putting our own take on it and updating it for contemporary family life.'

Nature played a major role, particularly when it came to selecting colours and materials. 'As Norwegians we love to be outside, but during winter we of course stay indoors quite a lot, so we like to bring nature inside and preserve it as much as possible,' Kine says.

TONE ON TONE

Matt beige walls showcase the southerly light in the living area (*right*). The furniture mixes clean-lined bamboo and soft bouclé upholstery, with an array of lighter and darker neutrals adding interest and depth. The arched wall lamp is by Belgian duo Muller Van Severen for Valerie Objects. Artworks on display include a trio of draped canvasses set in clay by Danish artist Sarah Kvejborg and framed reliefs woven from paper cord.

ARTFUL DISPLAY

The living-area walls are adorned with handmade artworks and accessories that incorporate natural materials, colours and shapes (*this page*). These include a plate with a swirling glaze that echoes the wider palette and a pebble-shaped wall vase sculpted by Copenhagen-based ceramicist Viki Weiland and filled with dried seedheads.

STATEMENT LIGHTING

A recessed alcove in the living area has been put to good use with bamboo display shelves and cupboard doors that fold open to reveal a concealed TV (*below*). Organically shaped pendant lamps made from fully compostable recycled paper add further natural texture, as well as zoning the sitting and dining spaces (*right*).

'I like pale, neutral tones and natural materials, which create a harmonious atmosphere and interact beautifully with the sunlight.'

The end palette encompasses subtle off-whites, greys and beiges alongside richer browns. Many of them were drawn from the different finishes available for bamboo, a signature material for former environmental geographer Kine and architect Kristoffer. The pair established Ask og Eng in 2016 after struggling to find a stylish, responsibly made kitchen system for their first apartment and now use it in most of their designs. 'Bamboo is beautiful and very durable, but it's also a sustainable choice,' Kine explains. 'It's actually a type of grass and it grows much faster than trees, without the need for any pesticides or artificial fertilizers.

FAMILY HUB

A custom-made island unit acts as a room divider between the living area and the kitchen, its slim legs ensuring it resembles a piece of furniture rather than dominating the space (*this page*). 'It's where we spend time with our two boys and hang out with friends and family when they come to visit,' says Kine. 'It also has a special kind of magic on weekend mornings, when everyone else is still asleep and I can enjoy a quiet moment with a cup of coffee.'

DECORATIVE DETAILS

The kitchen walls are painted in the same soft beige as the rest of the living space, but here with a limewash effect for subtle texture (*left*). An open shelf displays more artisan pieces, including hand-stitched abstract renderings of landscapes. The marble and onyx wall lamps were carved in the Mexican city of Tecali de Herrera and inspired by the stone masks of the ancient Teotihuacan civilization (*below*).

It's ready to be harvested within four to six years and absorbs more carbon dioxide during its growth than is released during production, meaning it's carbon-neutral over its complete life cycle.'

Indeed, bamboo forms a cohesive thread throughout the house, often in combination with other natural materials such as stone, linen and paper. The kitchen, for example, combines chocolate-stained bamboo fronts with stonework surfaces and limewashed walls – an elegant tonal scheme, with light and dark hues united by an underlying warmth.

On the other side of the island is an open-plan living area, created by relocating the staircase to the centre of the house. Here, a low-slung sofa and angular tables made from bamboo are offset by pieces with more organic silhouettes.

PRACTICAL STORAGE

To one side of the kitchen is a small walk-in pantry, where food shelves, the fridge-freezer and small appliances such as the coffee machine can be hidden from view (*this page*). It's one of many instances of cleverly integrated storage, which forms a common theme across almost every room in the house.

WORKING FROM HOME

Pale grey walls form an ideal backdrop in the dining room, which also functions as an office and meeting venue (*opposite*). Built-in cupboards mean business items can quickly be cleared away to turn it back into a family space. A desk is positioned by the window to catch the north-facing light (*this page*). The grid-like pattern of the bamboo shelving is enlivened by an undulating, ribbon-like candleholder and a vintage lamp shaped like a shell.

These curvaceous forms include an upholstered bouclé daybed and a mushroom-shaped lamp finished with a coat of lime plaster.

The rest of the downstairs is taken up by a dining room centred around an expansive bamboo table. It doubles as a home office and as an Ask og Eng meeting space, so versatility is key. The walls are painted in a delicate cloud-like grey – a quiet, unassuming hue that suits focused work sessions, client consultations, team catch-ups and relaxed family meals alike.

Nestled under the rafters above and arranged around a landing that acts as a cosy snug, the bedrooms and bathroom are simply furnished to ensure a supremely restful mood. The principal bedroom is especially appealing,

NEST SPACE

The upstairs landing has been repurposed as a snug (*left*). Wall-hung cupboards make the most of the awkward space beneath the rafters, their sleek lines offset by the rounded form of the sofa (another Ask og Eng creation). Similar curves appear in the sheepskin-covered Ingeborg armchair, designed by Danish great Flemming Lassen in 1940 (*right*).

with exposed beams, recycled-paper pendant lamps and a wide upholstered headboard that blends into the wall. ‘Our intention was to keep visual noise to a bare minimum, with hushed colours and soft textiles that encourage rest and sleep,’ says Kine.

She, Kristoffer and their sons now spend much of the time in Mallorca and open the house up to visitors as a showcase for their designs while they’re away, but it still functions as their family base whenever they’re back in Norway. ‘This house is somewhere we return to again and again, and it always gives us a sense of peace,’ Kine concludes. ‘It’s a place where we can disconnect from the hustle and bustle of running our own business, relax and feel completely at home.’

A QUIET OASIS

The muted colour palette and understated furniture in the principal bedroom keep the emphasis firmly on the high ceiling and gnarled beams above (*left and opposite*). In the corner is a rattan-backed Faaborg chair – a Scandinavian design classic created by Kaare Klint in 1914 for the purpose of contemplating artwork in Denmark's Faaborg Museum (*below*). It is a perfect match for this calming space.

OUR INTENTION WAS TO KEEP VISUAL NOISE TO A BARE MINIMUM, WITH HUSHED COLOURS AND SOFT TEXTILES THAT ENCOURAGE REST AND SLEEP

RAISING THE ROOF

The compact guest bedroom is painted in an airy off-white that creates a feeling of spaciousness beneath the low sloping ceiling (*opposite*). Both it and the principal bedroom feature folding shutters made from surplus planks of the pale ash flooring that runs throughout the house – an imaginative and sustainable way to use up leftover materials.

HOME SPA

Bamboo cupboards, bronze taps/faucets and a Norwegian granite counter with an integrated sink create a spa-like feel in the bathroom, in which a three-quarter-height internal wall screens the shower and WC (*left*). A mirror made from hand-turned wooden bobbins – a modern take on 17th-century spool furniture by British maker Alfred Newall – adds a playful touch. Camouflaged within the wooden panelling at the back is a secret door to a utility/laundry room (*above*).

CREATIVE COLOUR

As you step into the home of Charlie Davis, her partner Piers and their two young sons Herbie and Morley, the first things you notice are the hallway's orange doors and sunshine-yellow ceiling. They're just two examples of an artistic and at times surprising use of nature-inspired colour that runs throughout this double-fronted villa in the seaside town of Hastings, south-east England.

A WARM WELCOME

Charlie is a big fan of introducing colour via ceilings. In the hallway, a joyful yellow creates an uplifting, cheerful mood and sets the tone for the rest of the house (*above*). It also draws the eye upwards, emphasizing the building's lofty Victorian proportions. Incorporating part of the former dining room, the snug is fairly large but still feels cosy thanks to the Light Buff paint by Little Greene (*opposite*).

The family moved here from Brighton in 2020, attracted by the vibrant culture and coastal charm. 'It's like Brighton was 20 years ago,' explains Charlie. 'There are lots of shops and restaurants opening up, and there's a big festival and music scene. But it's also a working fishing port with traditional net huts, narrow lanes and boats being hauled up onto the beach with their catch.' The once-grand Victorian house, meanwhile, offered Charlie and Piers the top-to-bottom renovation project they were seeking.

'It was extremely run-down,' Charlie recalls. 'We had to do everything: rewiring, replumbing, replastering, restoring the floorboards and sash windows, replacing lost ceiling roses and cornicing/molding and installing a new kitchen and bathrooms. We also reconfigured the layout, adding an extension and opening things up so that you can see all the way through to the garden from the front door. With a one-year-old and a newborn in tow it was a huge undertaking, but we were determined to give the house the love it deserved.'

When it came to the decor, Charlie and Piers's aim was to reflect their personal taste and celebrate the building's character, while at the same time offering versatile photography backdrops for Charlie's work as a creative director and stylist. 'I had to balance my business head and my family head, as I knew we were going to open the house up as a photoshoot location but that it would also be our home,' she explains. 'Our style is natural and organic, with lots of warmth and texture, and we wanted the spaces to be homely yet uncluttered. Luckily Piers is an art fabricator and has a technical mind, so we could work together to find a way to achieve the look we wanted within our budget.'

ON THE LEVEL

The kitchen used to sit at the same level as the rest of the house, but Charlie and Piers decided to lower the floor, bringing it down to the height of the garden to maximize the leafy view and indoor-outdoor connection (*this page*). Terracotta tiles on the steps from the hallway provide texture and establish a link with the pink and ochre hues used elsewhere in the house.

A SENSE OF PLACE

The dining table sits in a new extension whose black timber cladding was inspired by the fishing-net huts on Hastings beach (*opposite*). Exposed ceiling joists discreetly separate the area from the kitchen and create a gently cocooning feel. Large picture windows mean the space almost seems to merge with the garden beyond, and there's a long built-in bench for storage.

CLEAN LINES

Charlie and Piers chose understated kitchen units with a grid-like pattern from Sussex-based Custom Fronts (*right*). 'We like the uniform, linear look, as it lends a calm simplicity to the busiest room in the house,' Charlie explains. The mix of brown and black-stained oak adds interest, while open shelving enables the couple to bring in shape and colour through ceramics and other accessories.

Colour is a key aspect of the resulting scheme, with subtle neutrals alongside stronger hues that take their cue from various aspects of the natural world. 'I like deep, muted tones – calming colours rather than anything too bright,' says Charlie. 'We have used bold colours in the house but we didn't want them to be overwhelming, so we've mostly kept them to ceilings, doors, furniture and artwork.'

As well as the hallway, this approach is particularly apparent in the snug. Here, panelled walls are painted in a honeyed shade that hovers between beige and ochre, and offset by thick burnt-orange velvet curtains, a forest-green sofa, a blue lacquered side table and a wood-and-cane easy chair upholstered in a delicate, blossom-like pink.

Other rooms are decorated in airy white but still incorporate flamboyant splashes of colour in their furniture and decorative accessories. The eclectic mix in the main living room, for example, includes a yellow sideboard/credenza, sky-blue armchairs and coral-pink accents.

In the kitchen, minimalist black and brown oak units are paired with eye-catching ceramics and towering potted plants. 'I like furniture that's a talking point – something a bit different – and mixing items of different eras, styles, textures and colours,' Charlie states. 'There are love-it-or-hate-it pieces all over the house, but they all mean something to us.'

The clever use of colour continues upstairs, where the main bedroom and its open-plan en-suite were formed by knocking two smaller rooms into one. Both are painted in a soothing dusky pink that brings to mind sunset skies and baked adobe – the perfect hue for a space dedicated to rest and relaxation. The wall behind the bathtub, however, has been stripped back to the plaster to create a textural focal point. 'We had bare plaster in our last house, and after spending four years renovating that place, I thought I'd never be able to look at it again!' Charlie says with a laugh. 'But the original lime-plastered wall here was just too beautiful to cover up. It took hours and hours to peel off the wood-chip wallpaper that was hiding it, but it was worth the effort.'

It certainly was. Imaginative yet harmonious, Charlie and Piers's home is a testament to the power of colour to influence mood, accentuate architectural features and draw the outside in. It also demonstrates the wealth of creative possibilities when it comes to building a palette, from small touches to big statements – proof that painting the walls is far from the only option.

OLD MEETS NEW

The living room reflects Charlie's love of mixing items from different eras and adding colour in unusual ways. The 1980s lacquered sideboard/credenza is from Sideshow, a Hastings shop that sources postmodernist designs from the USA, and the artwork above it is by Italian painter Francesco D'Adamo (*above*). The 1960s sofa is another Sideshow find (*opposite*). To its side is a glass Soho Home lamp – one of several coral-pink accents dotted around the space.

BRANCH LIBRARY

THE BRIGHT SIDE

Double doors in the living room frame views of the outside (*this page*). The blue vintage chairs came from Ode Interiors in nearby St Leonards-on-Sea, and the glass coffee table belonged to Piers's mother. A large tufted rug from Morocco adds texture and brings the various pieces together.

COLOUR IS A KEY ASPECT OF THE RESULTING SCHEME, WITH SUBTLE NEUTRALS ALONGSIDE STRONGER HUES THAT TAKE THEIR CUE FROM VARIOUS ASPECTS OF THE NATURAL WORLD

FAMILY RETREAT

In the snug, sumptuous velvet fabrics in bold hues add warmth and texture, whether used for curtains or upholstery (*opposite*). Charlie and Piers added a touch of period sophistication by installing wall panelling. The simple geometric design is highlighted by the ochre-toned paintwork.

REFINED RUSTICITY

The guest bedroom is decorated in Keim Colourwash paint, which creates a limewash effect with just one coat (*above left and above*). The textured finish is combined with half-height panelling, a jute rug, a sculptural granite-based Bowler side table from HAY and a laid-back canvas-and-steel easy chair for a look that is relaxed yet elegant.

IN THE PINK

The walls and woodwork/trim in the main bedroom are painted in Little Greene's Masquerade – a soft, powdery pink that is warm, restful and far from sugary (*left*). The colour is offset perfectly by green plants and a walnut chest of drawers/dresser edged in brass.

CONSIDERED CONTRASTS

A fitted wardrobe/closet with fluted doors divides the bedroom from the en-suite beyond (*opposite right and this page*). A minimalist stone-resin basin and sleek egg-shaped bathtub create a beautiful juxtaposition with the rough plaster and ornate cornicing/molding. In the shower, glossy pink Zellige tiles from Morocco are combined with grey marble-effect porcelain from Mandarin Stone for a textural contrast. 'For me, this space is the perfect balance of luxury and earthiness,' says Charlie.

MATERIALS AND TEXTURE

Natural materials create a powerful, multisensory connection with nature. They bring tactile and visual texture that we perceive through touch and sight, and they can affect the acoustics and even the scent of a space.

Our reaction to natural materials is both psychological and physical. Research has demonstrated that the higher the ratio of them in our surroundings, the more comfortable we feel and the lower our pulse rate. There's even some evidence to indicate that we sleep better in beds made from natural materials rather than synthetic ones.

But what counts as a natural material? Put simply, it's one that is found in nature and requires minimal intervention to be usable. A tree, for example, can be turned into timber for furniture with little treatment. Most metals, on the other hand, are drawn from the natural world but undergo such heavy processing that the end result bears scant resemblance to the starting point. The exceptions are native ores such as copper, which occur naturally in a usable form, and simple alloys such as brass and bronze, which have been made since ancient times. These can lend their beautiful patinas to biophilic schemes.

Natural materials encompass wood, stone, rattan, cane, bamboo and clay, as well as fibres such as flax, cotton, silk and wool. You may assume that they're most suited to rustic interiors, but there are plenty of options if your taste veers more towards the smart and the polished. Look to marble, granite and travertine, and select wood and ceramics with a smooth finish. The construction of natural fabrics can be used to showcase your personal style, too. For a relaxed effect, choose loose weaves and frayed edges; for something more refined, opt for tighter structures and neat seams.

FURNITURE AND ACCESSORIES
These offer endless possibilities for introducing natural materials and texture in a way that fits your space, budget and style (*opposite and above*). And if you rent your home, they may be your main tool. That doesn't mean avoiding the man-made completely, and even small touches – a wool throw, an earthenware vase – can have an impact. You needn't even buy anything new, as you can give existing pieces a natural twist through upcycling projects such as reupholstering headboards and chairs in linen or sanding back painted furniture to reveal the wood beneath.

WALLS, FLOORS AND CEILINGS

These are the largest surface areas in any space and the materials you select for them have a major impact.

You may be able to peel walls back to expose sections of stone, timber or plaster; if not, you can introduce natural texture through cladding, panelling or tiles. If you want to keep your walls plain, choose paints made from natural pigments and binders. Not only are they better for your health, your home and the environment, they bring a subtle chalkiness that's lacking with synthetic formulas. For more texture, try limewash paint applied in feathered brushstrokes (*above left*).

Underfoot, options include flagstones (*above right*), wooden boards (*below left*) or terracotta tiles. Cork is an increasingly popular choice thanks to its eco credentials and insulating properties. Some of these materials are even suitable for alfresco use, allowing you to enhance the indoor-outdoor connection by extending the flooring to terraces and patios. If you prefer carpet, seek out designs made from wool, sisal, jute, coir or seagrass (*below right*). They are often incredibly durable, meaning they're suitable for even high-traffic areas. For those who rent or don't have the budget for major changes, you can use rugs woven from these fibres to introduce natural texture to floors.

TEXTURAL VARIETY

Natural settings contain layers of different texture – just think of the glossy leaves, spongy moss and gnarled bark of a forest. By extension, interiors that are dominated by a single material will likely appear flat and lifeless, so introduce dashes of contrast – rough with smooth, soft with hard, matt with shiny – into your home (*above*).

It's particularly important to ensure that rooms with lots of hard surfaces also contain some softer, sound-absorbing elements such as curtains or upholstery. Overly echoey spaces have been proven to heighten stress levels and only contribute to the disconnect between the built environment and the natural world.

A SENSE OF PLACE

Biophilic design is about building a relationship not only with nature but also with our specific geographical setting. This creates a sense of belonging – the comforting feeling of being rooted in the place we call home. Using materials that reflect the local landscape, culture and history is an easy way to achieve this, whether they form the core of your decor or appear alongside influences from elsewhere (*below*). Even if you live in a city, there may be a local vernacular – perhaps a regional brick or traditional fabric – that you can reference.

CHARACTER STUDY

A deep respect for natural materials runs throughout the West Country home of interior designer Gemma Tucker and her husband Mark, a property investor.

Relocating from London to south-west England in search of a slower pace of life for themselves and their children, Tilly, aged 10, and George, seven, the couple fell for the charms of a listed Regency farmhouse on the Wiltshire-Somerset border.

'It has such a sense of history, yet it sits well with the pared-back, contemporary style of decor that we prefer,' Gemma explains. 'And I could see that, with a few changes, the floor plan offered everything we hoped to have – spaces that would be useful day-to-day, spread over two floors only. Many similar-sized houses that we viewed had three storeys, and I felt the top one would end up largely mothballed.'

Once a simple two-up, two-down cottage, the house had been extended several times over the years to incorporate adjacent agricultural buildings. It required further work to make it suitable for modern family life, but Gemma and Mark ensured that all updates stayed true to its character. 'We wanted to create a calm, cosy home that pays homage to the house's architecture, using materials that are in keeping with the local vernacular and the surrounding countryside.'

First on the agenda was optimizing the light, layout and flow ('always my starting point as a designer,' says Gemma), and the couple enlisted the help of historic building specialists Mark Wray Architects to achieve consent for the alterations. Much of their inspiration came from the Francis Gallery, set in a restored townhouse in nearby Bath, and the Babylonstoren hotel and farm in South Africa's Cape Winelands. Although very different from one another, they each incorporate the minimalist style that Gemma and Mark are drawn towards while honouring their location and roots.

UPSTAIRS, DOWNSTAIRS

On the upstairs landing, Gemma has displayed some of her most cherished pieces, including a wall hanging that she bought long ago and a brass mobile that catches the light and sends reflections dancing across the walls (*above*). Much more than a place to pass through, the hallway below is somewhere the family lingers, often playing board games at the table (*opposite*). The buttery hue of Paint & Paper Library's Stone III evokes the Bath stone of the building's exterior, while the flagstones replicate the flooring that would have been used here in the 18th century. The artwork above the fireplace is by Gemma's sister Mimi Zouch.

HEART OF THE HOME

The kitchen and adjacent dining area have become the family's favourite spaces (*left and opposite*). 'They're flooded with natural light and feel very peaceful,' says Gemma. 'I love to watch the sunrise over the fields in the mornings and the sunset through the windows on the other side at the end of the day. This is also where we welcome friends and enjoy long meals and laughter. In summer, with the doors open, the inside and outside feel like one connected space.'

The biggest change was moving the kitchen from a small, low-ceilinged room to a vaulted former cowshed, which the previous owner had joined to the main house to use as a library. Taking her cue from the exposed oak trusses, Gemma introduced sawn-oak flooring and travertine worktops, with limewash paint on the walls. Minimalist units and a long island in blackened oak add an element of modernity.

The space beyond the kitchen has become a convivial dining area, with partial walls and a change in level creating two distinct zones while preserving the sense of openness and connection. Here, Gemma and Mark added a panoramic window gazing out over the fields and commissioned a bespoke oak table and cushioned bench that maximize seating without blocking movement through the space. Hanging above are a pair of hand-crafted crochet pendant lights sourced from Marrakech-based Hamimi, with a low black sideboard/credenza along the opposite wall echoing the kitchen units to form a cohesive thread. At the far end, an oak staircase and elegant black handrail twist up to a guest bedroom and snug tucked into the roof space above.

In the 18th-century core of the house, Gemma and Mark reinstated traditional shutters to accentuate the tall sash windows. They also removed the ceiling above the hallway and landing, creating a lofty space open to the rafters and bathed in natural light from a pair of new roof lights. The upstairs layout was then rejigged, with two small en-suites making way for larger children's rooms and a main suite encompassing a bedroom, dressing area and bathroom.

SHELF APPEAL

Planning restrictions meant Gemma and Mark had to work with the existing windows when designing their new kitchen (*this page*). They eschewed wall-hung cupboards and tall cabinetry in favour of base units only – a decision that had the added advantage of enhancing the calm, airy atmosphere. Open shelves provide display space for plants, artwork and ceramics, and there is additional storage in the adjoining pantry.

CALM AND COSY

The living room is painted in At The Bay by Atelier Ellis – a gentle green that brings the outdoors in (*this page*). Its grey undertones are warmed by a golden velvet sofa and dark wooden coffee table, with a mohair rug and linen cushions providing layers of inviting texture. Opposite the sofa is a Crown easy chair from Stockholm-based furniture company Massproductions, which adds a sculptural element.

PERFECTLY IMPERFECT

The study features the graceful curves of a Kidney desk from Fred Rigby Studio and some of Gemma's treasured ceramics (*above*). 'I love to observe the hand of the maker in beautifully imperfect pieces,' she says. The former kitchen is now a boot room, with olive-green walls, simple oak cabinets and a flagstone floor (*opposite*). Soft white paint on the beamed ceiling makes it seem higher than it is.

'WE WANTED TO CREATE A CALM, COSY HOME THAT PAYS HOMAGE TO THE HOUSE'S ARCHITECTURE, USING MATERIALS THAT ARE IN KEEPING WITH THE LOCAL VERNACULAR'

TEXTURED WALLS

The natural ingredients and stone-like texture of limewash paint are inherently biophilic. It's used to beautiful effect in the guest bedroom, where it's offset by ochre and russet accents that reflect the colour of the old beams (*above*). A linen curtain in the foreground separates this bedroom from the snug, creating versatile spaces that can be opened up or closed off as needed (*right*).

SLEEP SANCTUARY

The main bedroom overlooks the garden, with windows on two sides (*top left and above right*). Putty-pink walls (Cotta by Atelier Ellis) create a serene feel, with indigo and ochre accents adding depth. Gemma upholstered the headboard herself using a raw organic cotton, and introduced further texture with a velvet cushion, a woollen rug and handmade ceramic lamps. The corridor to the bedroom serves as a dressing area (*above left*). Linen drapes take the place of wardrobe/closet doors that would block the window when open.

PAST AND PRESENT

Gemma and Mark's en-suite is set in what used to be a bedroom. One alcove is taken up by a painted wooden cabinet that provides a mix of closed storage and display shelves (*left*). A sliding door maximizes space (*above*). Dark marble sinks and brassware add an air of contemporary luxury, while the roll-top tub and custom-made washstands give a nod to the house's age (*opposite*).

For the flooring in the older section of the property, Gemma chose flagstones and reclaimed pine boards in a dark chocolate stain, both materials that are in keeping with the building and the local landscape. Linen drapes, jute rugs, lantern-like paper pendant lights and clay vases in organic shapes add further natural textures and soften the clean lines of the Georgian architecture.

The colour palette, too, references nature, with muted greens, earthy pinks, inky blue accents and stony neutrals that connect the house to its surroundings. 'All the colours feel restful and sit as a backdrop rather than dominating the space,' says Gemma. The use of handmade paint with natural pigments brings subtle depth and allows the walls of the building to breathe.

The result of the renovation is a relaxed, comfortable and functional family home with quiet, considered interiors that celebrate the 18th-century building, its unique story and its location, hidden away among the fields. 'The house makes me feel relaxed and like myself,' Gemma concludes. 'It's easy to live in, and the light and flow have improved dramatically. We feel so lucky to be the custodians of this beautiful place.'

CIRCULAR THINKING

Designer Nina Woodcroft dedicates her working life to creating elegant, textural spaces with minimal environmental impact, so natural and sustainable materials were always going to figure prominently in the transformation of her own home in north London.

Nina, whose studio Nina + Co was responsible for the interiors of the UK's first zero-waste restaurant among other projects, bought the 1970s semi-detached house with her partner Joe Hutchinson in early 2023. Determined to turn what was then a cold, leaky and soulless property into a warm, energy-efficient retreat for themselves and their young son Arlo, they commissioned architecture firm ROAR to help. The brief: to make the most of the existing footprint without extending, using natural, local or recycled materials wherever possible.

'It was something of an unusual move,' says Nina. ' Many people would have built over the side return or done a loft conversion, but we wanted to focus our time and budget on improving what we already had – a quiet protest against demolition culture.'

STATEMENT PIECE

With its tactile wood, generous proportions and rounded bullnose edges, the kitchen island forms a striking yet graceful focal point (*right*). Both it and the cabinets behind were made from responsibly sourced British timber. 'It feels like a privilege to be surrounded by grown materials that have had a rich past life,' explains Nina.

First, the rickety porch and a small garage were incorporated into the main structure, draughty windows were replaced with high-performance triple glazing and an air-source heat pump and ventilation system were installed. The entire house was then wrapped in cork – a highly insulating and carbon-negative material, harvested from regenerative forests in Portugal without any damage to the trees themselves.

Cork was also chosen for the flooring inside, with any lifted floorboards retained and repurposed as ceiling cladding in certain sections of the house. The walls were covered in lime plaster, which has been left exposed to showcase its texture and sealed with a VOC-free transparent glaze. On the walls that were inaccessible from the outside, this was mixed with cork granules to replicate the insulative properties of the exterior finish.

Laid out with busy family life in mind, the once-fragmented downstairs now consists of one large, flowing space, with dedicated zones for cooking, reading, sharing meals and, adds Nina, 'even dancing'. At its heart is the kitchen.

BRANCHING OUT

Nina made a patchwork café-style curtain for the kitchen using swatches of natural fabrics that she had accumulated over the years (*above left*). Strings of pine cones and dried orange slices bring nature into the space. The cabinets are made of Douglas fir from Scotland (*above*). Nina also created a sculptural lighting installation above the island by wiring branches from the garden to a suspended LED strip (*opposite*).

Here, the star feature is a chunky island with rounded, child-friendly edges. This was crafted by local joinery company Craftworks Productions from a rescued London plane tree that had been felled in Soho Square by Westminster Council. The cabinets behind were made using tri-ply board from British-grown Douglas fir and paired with a practical recycled-plastic work surface that sets up a beautiful contrast with the visible knots and grain of the wood.

The curves of the island are replicated in the custom cabinetry in the smaller of two sitting areas, located to one side of the kitchen. A space created with coffee, reading and listening to music in mind, it features a mix of open display shelves and closed storage cupboards built from kitchen offcuts, their rounded end section extending around a corner to soften the angles of the internal walls.

The focus on natural materials and reuse continues in the furniture and decorative accessories, many of which are vintage. Some of the pieces in the dining area and the main sitting area, which overlook the garden at the rear of the house, belonged to Nina's parents; others were sourced from online marketplaces. Rattan, linen and cane appear regularly, both here and in the bedrooms above, as do items made from waste products by local designers. Dotted here and there are natural finds such as pine cones and bare branches, together with houseplants in all manner of varieties and sizes.

It's perhaps no surprise that Nina and Joe's home has been shortlisted for several awards, and a year after the works were completed, the couple are enjoying its calmness and comfort. 'I feel very lucky to inhabit a space that I know inside out, and it gives me peace of mind to know that most elements can one day be returned to the earth without causing harm,' says Nina. 'I hope sharing our experience encourages more people to explore natural materials – not just for our wellbeing now, but for the benefit of generations to come.'

A NEW LEASE OF LIFE

Timber ceiling cladding made from floorboards removed during the renovation adds cosiness to the rear of the downstairs, subtly differentiating the dining space and the main sitting area from the kitchen at the front (*opposite and below*). The red leather-and-chrome dining chairs belonged to Nina's parents, and the table was an eBay find. Nina and Joe have plans to grow climbing plants up the fence by the window, creating another green link between indoors and out.

URBAN JUNGLE

Partially enclosed by the staircase on one side and opening to the garden on the other, the main sitting area is furnished with a vintage 1970s sofa and matching ottoman whose green velvet upholstery echoes the leafy planting outside (*this page*). Nina and Joe also have an impressive collection of indoor plants, which form a running connection with nature throughout the house.

WASTE NOT, WANT NOT

Cupboards, drawers and shelving built from kitchen offcuts provide a home for books, vinyl and decorative objects in the smaller sitting area (*this page*). These include a bowl made from mycelium – a tactile, biodegradable material formed from the root structure of mushrooms, which Nina has used in several client projects.

NATURAL WARMTH

The space, occupying what was once a porch and garage, is illuminated from above by a skylight (*opposite*). Cork flooring runs across the ground floor, providing thermal and acoustic insulation in the open-plan space. 'The cork is so warm, practical and forgiving,' says Nina. It's also a highly sustainable and renewable material: cork bark is harvested without harming the tree beneath and regrows each time, while the forests are biodiverse ecosystems that absorb significant amounts of carbon.

A TACTILE MIX

The principal bedroom features a rattan headboard, glossy-leafed plants and linen bedding in a sun-baked terracotta pink (*left and opposite*). The organically shaped bedside table/nightstand was crafted from leftover plasterboard/drywall by Walthamstow-based designer-maker Byron, who works mainly with waste materials and found objects, and almost looks like an extension of the textured wall behind.

RATTAN, LINEN AND CANE APPEAR REGULARLY, TOGETHER WITH HOUSEPLANTS IN ALL VARIETIES AND SIZES

The Monocle Guide
to Good Business
Openhouse

SHAPE AND PATTERN

Mimicking the shapes and patterns found in the natural world is a core component of biophilic design. The official term for it is biomorphism, which makes it sound more complicated than it is. It's actually a very simple way to reference nature in your home, whatever its size, style and location. And it's a particularly effective one: studies have suggested that spaces which contain forms lifted from flora, fauna, landscapes and geology are not only more visually appealing, they also reduce stress levels and improve our cognitive performance.

BIOMORPHIC SHAPES

Curves, rounded shapes and flowing forms are prevalent throughout the natural world. As a result we're inherently drawn to them, associating them with comfort, relaxation and inclusivity. Most people, for example, will perceive curved tables and seating arrangements as more inviting and less confrontational than rectangular ones (*opposite and above*).

Curves and irregular shapes soften the straight lines and sharp angles that normally characterize the built environment, introducing fluidity to spaces that would otherwise appear static. They can be incorporated through architectural features such as archways, columns and sweeping staircases, through furniture, cabinetry, rugs and even through small details such as ceramics and lamps.

That isn't to say that you should shy away from lines and angles altogether – and unless you live in a home with curved walls and ceilings, they're hard to avoid. But breaking them up with a few organic forms here and there will instantly make a space feel more welcoming.

BIOMORPHIC PATTERNS

Patterns and repeating forms are everywhere in nature, too, from the spots and stripes of animal markings to the ripples created by wind blowing across sand and water. Some are soft and sinuous, others more precise and geometric – just think of the concentric circles of tree rings and the repeating hexagons of snowflakes, honeycombs and basalt rock columns.

The patterns of the natural world can be replicated in numerous ways, and you can make them as eye-catching or as subtle as you want. Go big with patterned wallpaper, upholstery and rugs (*above left*), or take a more subtle approach with decorative accessories and artworks (*above right and below left*). Biomorphic patterns can even be introduced through the layout of floor and wall tiles or the structure of woven rattan furniture (*below right*).

SYMMETRY AND ASYMMETRY

Nature encompasses symmetry and asymmetry, with mirror-image shapes and highly structured patterns alongside organic and imperfect forms. What's more, we humans respond to both, associating symmetry with beauty (we are, after all, largely symmetrical creatures ourselves) but finding too much of it in a space imposing and off-putting. As a result, symmetry and asymmetry each have a role to play in biophilic design, and finding a balance between the two will make for a much more comfortable and harmonious home. The display shown here, for example, has a symmetrical circular vase with an asymmetrical dried stem and a wavy candleholder (*below*). It evokes the diversity, complexity and dynamism of the natural world – and serves as an important reminder of just how amazing this planet of ours really is.

FRACTALS AND SPIRALS

Fractals – intricate patterns made up of shapes that repeat themselves at different scales – are particularly common in the natural world, appearing in pine cones, fern fronds, leaf veins, river deltas and tree branches, to name but a few examples. In fact, they form such a major part of our visual experience that we find them instinctively pleasing, displaying a preference for them from early childhood.

We also seem to be highly attuned to patterns based around the Fibonacci sequence and the golden ratio. The sequence is a series of numbers where each is the sum of the two that precede it (1, 1, 2, 3, 5, 8, 13, 21, 34 etc.). If you divide any number in the sequence over five by the previous one, you get an answer very close to 1.618: the golden ratio. Both can be found time and time again in natural structures and living organisms that unfold in spirals, from seashells to the leaves of succulents to the petals of flowers such as hellebores (*above*).

Luckily, fractals and spirals are easy to bring into the home – either directly, through plants, blooms and foraged finds, or indirectly, through artworks, prints and accessories with natural motifs.

A PLAY ON NATURE

For proof that biophilic design isn't only the preserve of rustic interiors, look no further than the east London house of freelance interiors stylist and photographer Halima Mason. With its sculptural shapes, sleek materials and bursts of vibrant colour, it almost resembles a modern art gallery – but one that's full of warmth and soul, and inherently liveable.

Halima also works as a wholesale and residential projects manager for homeware retailer SCP. She and her husband Laurence, a British Sign Language interpreter, bought the Victorian terrace in 2023 after relocating from Manchester with their young son. Long drawn to minimalism, Halima's aim was to create a calm, uncluttered home with an imaginative twist. But rather than planning every corner of the interiors, she relied on her intuition to craft a series of beautifully unique spaces that reflects her style and story.

'Our previous house was very neutral, with lots of whites, beiges and creams,' she explains. 'I'm a minimalist through and through, but I decided with this place that I wanted to embrace colour. I've also developed a real love for art – and furniture that resembles art – so I focused on collecting pieces that I love without necessarily thinking about how they fit together within the scheme as a whole.'

First, however, the bones of the property required attention. 'It hadn't been touched for a few decades, so we had to rewire the whole place, strip away the dated fitted wardrobes/closets and carpet and redo all the floors, walls and ceilings,' Halima says. 'It needed a lot more work than we initially thought.'

The old-fashioned layout also necessitated some changes. The front and middle rooms had already been knocked through into one open-plan living area, but as is common in many terraces of the period, the bathroom was located at the rear of the downstairs. Halima and Laurence therefore demolished the wall between it and the kitchen, forming a long space with doors out to the garden behind.

SCULPTURAL SHAPES

Flowing forms feature in much of the furniture and accessories, some of which are artworks in their own right. One such piece is the Melt mirror by Bower Studios, which hangs above the sofa (*this page*). 'I saw it on a trip to New York and thought it was more like a sculpture than a mirror,' says Halima. Curves also appear in the iconic Roattino floor lamp, designed by Eileen Gray in 1931, and at the base of the side table by Danish studio Kristina Dam, where they soften the straight-sided steel.

TREASURED PIECES

The playful silhouette of a 1967 Flos Snoopy lamp sits on a tomato-red cube by Sabine Marcelis (*this page*). A floating-console display mixes contemporary design with personal items (*opposite*). The ultramarine wall unit is by Lisbon-based Util and the painting above is by Laurence's mother. The East African chungu pot belonged to Halima's late grandmother, who used it for cooking with fire. 'I can feel her legacy in the grooves and marks on the clay – it brings me so much joy to see it in my home.'

SANTA&COLE

REBORN BEAUTY

The origami-inspired coffee table in the sitting area was created by Spanish designer Patricia Urquiola for Italian marble company Budri and shows how natural materials can be introduced in surprising ways (*left and above*). It was made using broken fragments of stone from the Emilia earthquakes of May 2012, with the aim of finding new life amid destruction.

CURVES IN COMBINATION

The contrast between curved forms and straight lines is a defining feature of the dining area (*opposite*). The vintage Serenissimo table was designed by Lella and Massimo Vignelli and David Law in 1985, and sourced from London 20th-century furniture specialist Everything But The Dog. By the window is an Atollo lamp by Oluce, whose dome-like shape is repeated in the glass pendant hanging in the centre of the room.

They then divided one of the bedrooms into two to create a new bathroom upstairs and turned the cupboard beneath the stairs into a small guest WC.

When it came to furnishing the rejigged spaces, Halima focused on pieces she was instinctively drawn towards. The result is an artistic mix of curves and organic forms, offset by clean lines and geometric patterns. In the living room, for example, a rounded sofa and flowing mirror sit alongside a marble coffee table whose crisp angles were inspired by origami, while the dining table behind consists of a square sheet of glass that seems to float on circular column-like legs.

These striking design pieces are interspersed with cherished items that have personal meaning for the family. Many of the paintings are by Laurence's mother, Scottish artist Alison McBride, and dotted here and there are handmade East African heirlooms that hold childhood memories for Halima, who was born in Tanzania and moved to the UK when she was eight years old. There are also plenty of splashes of bold colour, with mint green, cobalt blue, lemon yellow and deep, earthy reds forming recurrent threads across multiple rooms.

Materials, too, play a major role in the overall look and feel of the house. Throughout, Halima has skilfully mixed man-made and natural surfaces, incorporating smooth glass and industrial steel alongside tactile wood, clay, stone and paper cord.

MIXED MATERIALS

In the kitchen, Halima paired stainless steel with Cipollino Ondulato Verde marble sourced from a local offcut supplier, setting up a contrast between the minimalist unit fronts and the swirling patterns of the worktops (*opposite and this page*). Checkerboard oak-block flooring adds another layer of materiality, while the green tones of the marble are picked up in the painted doorframe at one end of the room.

A LEGACY OF PASSIONATE CRAFTSMANSHIP

GARDEN VIEW

Created out of the former bathroom, the sitting area at the end of the kitchen is one of the family's favourite spaces (*opposite*). 'It's where we spend our mornings having breakfast together, and the large sliding doors bring the outside in,' Halima states. The marble coffee table and steel Drum F1 floor lamp from Minimalux reference the materials of the units and worktops. There are subtle natural analogues in the curves and tiger-motif upholstery of the daybed.

SMALL SPACE, BIG IMPACT

The deep burgundy that appears in various places around the house takes centre stage in the downstairs WC, which is painted in Chestnuts in the Park by Valspar (*right*). It's offset by a matt white basin and a marble splashback criss-crossed by striking red and ochre veins.

SLEEP NEST

The principal bedroom is a restful space in soft beiges and greens, but it nevertheless incorporates interesting forms (*this page*). The upholstered bed, designed by Philippe Malouin for SCP, gently curves inwards to create a comforting cocoon. Its rounded form is echoed in the April bedside table/nightstand by Finnish brand Nikari. On the wall is a Rondo mirror by Poland-based Zieta Studio, which combines highly polished steel with an irregular, dimpled surface.

NATURE AND NOSTALGIA

An embracing, cloud-like Puffy armchair by Faye Toogood makes a whimsical statement in the corner of the bedroom (*right*). The forest-green rug incorporates a geometric pattern often found in nature, while the small wooden stool was carved from Tanzanian mninga wood by Halima's grandfather (*below*). 'I can remember sitting on it as a child,' she says.

Marble is a particular favourite, featuring throughout on kitchen work surfaces, tables, lamp bases, bathroom splashbacks and more. 'It adds so much visual interest with its varying colours, textures and veins,' Halima says.

The natural references in the couple's home may not be immediately obvious, but they have a powerful impact. Not only do they bridge the gap between nature and the urban setting, they also contribute to the tranquil, inviting atmosphere. 'This house feels like a sanctuary,' concludes Halima. 'After being at work all day, it's a bubble away from everything – a space where we can truly relax.'

A PLACE FOR EVERYTHING

In the bedroom of Halima and Laurence's son, painted arches zone the sleeping area in a playful way (*right*). A custom-made unit from Tylko provides plenty of storage (*below and opposite*). It's paired with a Bollo armchair by Sweden-based Fogia, forming another example of the red-and-green, curves-and-lines combinations found throughout the house.

HALIMA FOCUSED ON PIECES SHE WAS INSTINCTIVELY DRAWN TOWARDS. THE RESULT IS AN ARTISTIC MIX OF CURVES AND ORGANIC FORMS, OFFSET BY CLEAN LINES AND GEOMETRIC PATTERNS

CURVE APPEAL

'Natural tones, textures and shapes are my go-to,' says interiors content creator Roxanne Hudson. They certainly take centre stage in her Leicester home in England's East Midlands, which combines a grounding autumnal palette with tactile materials, organic forms and nature-mimicking patterns.

Roxanne moved into the 1907-built terraced house with her dog Monty three and a half years ago and set about making it her own. 'It had previously been rented out to tenants for many years, so it was dated and in need of some TLC, but it had great potential,' she recalls. 'It didn't require any structural work other than in the bathroom, where the walls were so spongy I could put my finger through them! That meant I could largely focus on cosmetic updates and making it feel like a home. I always lean towards a calm, relaxing and earthy style, so I knew that was the direction I wanted to go in.'

For colour inspiration, Roxanne turned to her favourite season, autumn, introducing biscuit-like beiges, comforting terracottas, warm browns and umber-based greens that reference the fall landscape. Many of these hues are drawn from a collection she herself created for paint company Rust-Oleum and applied in unusual ways. The living room, for example, features half-painted walls that inject interest and vibrancy without dominating the decor. Both it and the bedroom above have darker ceilings that lend a sense of cosiness to the bright south-facing spaces, while the north-facing snug is a cocooning retreat decorated in a deep chestnut. And in Roxanne's home office, the floorboards are covered in tonal checkerboard squares – a geometric pattern that's found across the natural world, from the markings on beetles and butterflies to the petals of fritillary flowers.

HALF MEASURES

Roxanne has painted the lower half of the living-room walls in a pale beige called Still and the upper half in a dusky terracotta named Fired Clay, both from her collaboration with Rust-Oleum (*above and opposite*). It's a visual trick that adds warmth and depth to the space, and it evokes the wainscoting typically found in houses of this age. A gallery of abstract prints with rounded, organic shapes bisects the dividing line, blurring the visual boundary between the two halves. Curved forms also appear in the leaf-like Arum wall lamp from Danish brand Ferm Living, which was inspired by the plant of the same name.

SCANDIRUSTIC

NICHE INTEREST

Roxanne has made good use of an awkward arched niche in the living room, adding a green linen armchair and jute rug to create an inviting corner with a view of the window (*opposite*). The natural world is referenced in the irregular stripes of the blanket and the flowing shape of the mirror – one of several similar designs dotted throughout the house.

GOING DARK

The snug is just that – a cosy sanctuary painted in a warm reddish brown (*above and above right*). Organic forms offset the straight lines of the sofa, shelving and fireplace, featuring across ceramics, cushions, artworks and more. There are plenty of natural materials, too, with decorative baskets, stoneware vases and an undyed linen lampshade popping against the dark walls.

Counterbalancing the clean lines of the paint effects and the Edwardian architecture are fluid, rounded and irregular shapes. These appear across furniture, artworks, mirrors, lighting and smaller accessories such as vases and planters, as well as in wall hangings and blankets whose stripes evoke rippling water and wind-blown sand. 'They add softness and movement to spaces that might otherwise feel quite rigid,' Roxanne explains. 'They also draw the eye to different areas of the room, creating a sense of flow.'

Alongside these forms, Roxanne has introduced inviting layers of texture, with rattan lamps, jute rugs, woollen blankets and an array of different woods. She is particularly drawn to linen, which acts as a cohesive thread across armchairs, sofas, cushions and curtains. It even adorns the front of the chest of drawers/dresser, bedside tables/nightstands and wardrobe/armoire in the bedroom, adding appealing tactility to functional storage.

KITCHEN FACELIFT

Roxanne spruced up the existing kitchen by painting the units in a muted mid-brown with green undertones (*opposite*). She also covered the multicoloured mosaic splashback with tile paint, blending it into the new scheme while retaining its texture and tessellated pattern. Other updates included hiding the washing machine with a gingham curtain and laying terrazzo tiles on the worktop. 'It was much more cost-effective than replacing the entire thing, and I like the contrast with the visible strip of wood along the edge,' explains Roxanne.

WINDOW TABLE

Roxanne has turned the recessed kitchen window into a cushioned bench, maximizing space around the dining table (*left and above*). 'It's become one of my favourite spots in the house, and it gets the most beautiful morning light,' she says. A conical rattan pendant and jute rug define this area within the wider room. Behind the table is a custom-made pantry cupboard from local company Stapling Bespoke, painted the same colour as the walls and finished with gently curved brass handles from hardware supplier Corston Architectural Detail. Hooks and straw baskets add texture and further storage to the plain end panel.

HOME(LY) OFFICE

A checkerboard floor makes a statement in Roxanne's office (*above*). The dual colours share similar undertones, ensuring the overall look is harmonious rather than jarring. The darker of the two hues also covers the built-in cupboards and extends partway up the wall behind the desk, creating a defined work zone (*opposite*). A circular rug, an arched mirror and a side table hewn from a tree trunk balance out the space's strong vertical and horizontal lines.

COUNTERBALANCING THE CLEAN LINES OF THE EDWARDIAN ARCHITECTURE ARE FLUID, ROUNDED AND IRREGULAR SHAPES

FLOWER POETRY
CURATE

RIPPLE EFFECT

A large wall hanging – actually a repurposed throw – introduces a ripple-like pattern to the bedroom (*left and above*). It ties in perfectly with the soft grey-green of the ceiling and the beige of the bed linen and furniture, drawing the various elements of the room together. There are additional natural analogues in the shapes and textures of the ceramics, and in the floral motifs of the art print on the other side of the bed. The linen-fronted drawers are from Norwegian designer Magnus Pettersen's Marna collection for Heal's.

SEASONAL DISPLAY

A vase of autumnal foliage in the corner of the bedroom pays homage to the season that has inspired so much of Roxanne's decor (*opposite*). The bay window houses an inviting armchair – a favourite of Monty the dog – and another of the eye-catching mirrors that add organic shape to various spots around the house. Sheer linen curtains and slatted shutters help to filter the strong southerly light.

Terrazzo is another recurring element. A centuries-old composite material made from fragments of stone, marble or shell set in resin or cement, it offers a way to incorporate varied natural shapes in areas that require hard-wearing, durable and waterproof surfaces. Nowadays it's available as ready-made tiles, which Roxanne has used to beautiful effect. In her kitchen, they add a twist to the existing wooden worktops, and they can also be seen on the walls, floor and counter of the newly overhauled bathroom. 'They give a subtle hint of colour and pattern but they're not overpowering,' she says.

Roxanne is rightly proud of the home that she has single-handedly renovated. 'Breathing life back into older properties in a way that's sympathetic to their age and my own style is something of a passion – it gives me a sense of purpose,' she says. 'There are moments when I walk around this place and I can't quite believe it's mine – that I've created all this.'

TIMELESS TERRAZZO

In the bathroom, Roxanne has alternated terrazzo tiles with plain, adding colour and pattern without overwhelming the small space (*above left and above*). The terrazzo chips reflect the rich brown of the wooden vanity unit and the black of the shower frame and stool, creating a cohesive scheme. Roxanne has also added a linen shower curtain as well a glass screen. 'Probably controversial,' she laughs, 'but it makes the room feel softer and much less clinical. And it stops steam escaping, so it serves a practical purpose.'

LIGHT AND LIGHTING

Natural light is vital to our health and happiness. It encourages our bodies to produce Vitamin D, which supports our bones and immune system, and it increases levels of the mood-boosting hormone serotonin. It also plays a crucial role in regulating our circadian rhythm – our biological sleep-wake cycle.

Natural light is dynamic, varying in intensity, position and colour temperature over the course of 24 hours. During the daytime, it's brighter and cooler, encouraging the release of cortisol – the hormone that makes us feel energized and awake. In the late afternoon and evening, it becomes softer and warmer before fading out, suppressing cortisol and replacing it with sleep-inducing melatonin. A lack of natural light and overexposure to artificial light upsets this pattern, leading to fatigue, insomnia, depression and more. It's why many of us feel sluggish on dark winter mornings, and why sleep experts discourage the use of computer and phone screens, which emit blue-tinged light, in the hours before bed.

It's perhaps no surprise, then, that maximizing natural light – and ensuring that when we do have to resort to artificial light, it mimics the real thing as closely as possible – is a fundamental part of biophilic design.

EXTERNAL GLAZING

Investing in external glazing is a surefire way to increase natural light in your home (*opposite*). Skylights and roof lanterns are particularly effective, bringing in more than twice the amount of light as normal vertical windows. They're most commonly associated with loft rooms and kitchen extensions but also work brilliantly above desks, tables and stairwells. Another useful option is clerestory windows – strips of glazing fitted near the top of walls to let in light without compromising privacy (*above*). In either case, coatings can be added to the glass to cut out glare and prevent the spaces beneath from overheating.

WINDOW DRESSINGS

The way you dress your windows can make a big difference, too. If you want to maximize the natural light, ensure curtains hang from poles that exceed the width of the glass (so that they don't cover much of it when open) and position blinds/shades high enough above windows that they don't block light when raised. Swapping to semi-sheer fabrics also helps, and in bedrooms you can layer these with blackout blinds/shades for sleeping. In areas where you need privacy, slatted shutters, stick-on frosted film and café-style curtains, which cover the lower half of windows only, will stop prying eyes but allow light through (*below*).

Try not to place furniture directly in front of windows. Where this is unavoidable, choose slimline, low-profile or open-backed designs that obstruct as little light as possible.

BORROWED LIGHT

If you have a space with little or no natural light of its own, look for ways to borrow some from elsewhere. Replacing solid walls and doors with internal glazing lets light flow from one room to another, and this can work wonders in the dark central areas of terraced homes and apartments (*above*). Other options include adding glass ceilings or floors between different levels, swapping closed staircases for open designs and installing light tunnels – reflective tubes that channel sunrays from small glass domes on the roof. Even fitting fanlights (glazed panels) above doorways can help.

If you can't stretch to structural changes, then fear not. A well-placed mirror can bounce light towards a gloomy corner, as can reflective surfaces such as metal and polished stone – just make sure you don't go overboard and end up with a space that feels stark and echoey.

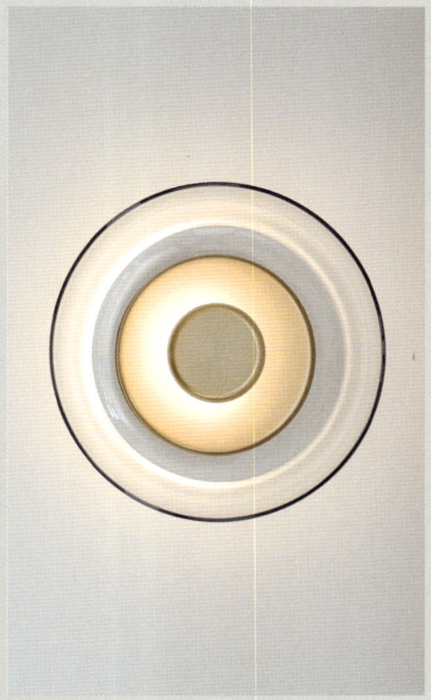

COLOUR TEMPERATURE

Altering the hue of artificial lighting to match the cycle of natural light will help your circadian rhythm stay on track (*above*). In the past, this entailed having different bulbs in different lamps, with cooler ones to keep you alert in the day and warmer ones to help you wind down in the evening – not ideal in multifunctional spaces where the dining table might double as your desk. Nowadays, you can buy smart bulbs that screw into existing fittings and enable you to change the temperature via an app. Some can even be programmed to adjust automatically and most are dimmable, removing the hassle of hardwiring dimmer switches into your walls.

Don't underestimate the calming power of candlelight, either. Its cosy glow is the perfect antidote to blue-toned daytime light, lowering our heart rate and signalling to our brains that it's time to relax.

LAYERED LIGHTING

Natural light comes from multiple directions, with direct sunrays, light reflected off water and diffused light filtered through clouds and trees. Layering artificial light sources so that you have a mix of wall, floor, table and pendant lamps dotted at different heights around a room will replicate this, as will introducing a balance between targeted task lighting, softer ambient lighting and inviting pockets of light that draw you towards certain areas or features (*above*). Portable battery-powered lamps are useful, as you can move them wherever needed; they're also handy for corners without a plug socket/power outlet, and anywhere you don't want trailing cables. Make as much of your lighting as possible dimmable so that you can dial the intensity up or down according to the time of day.

LIGHT AND BRIGHT

Tired of city life and yearning for a slower pace, export documentation manager Marloes Etman and her husband Bart, who works in IT, moved from Dordrecht to a small village in the Dutch province of North Brabant. The setting, amid rolling fields and forests, offered the couple the rural tranquillity they had long dreamed of, but initially they were far from enamoured with the 1970s farmhouse they ended up buying.

'It was still in its original state, and not what we were searching for,' Marloes recalls. 'The kitchen, bathroom and living spaces all needed a complete makeover, and it certainly wasn't love at first sight! We knew it would be a lot of work, but it was detached and the location was exactly what we needed, so we decided to go for it.'

The couple got the keys in 2021 and set about turning the dark and dated interior into a modern, light-filled home. Marloes had a clear vision: bright yet cosy, with an earthy, nature-inspired mood that would stand the test of time. But she also wanted the house itself to guide the renovation. 'I believe an interior should grow over time, and I knew we needed to get to know the various spaces before making firm decisions,' she explains. 'How does the light change during the day? What is the best view? Where do we like to sit, eat and relax? Only by being in the house could we answer these questions, and our ideas evolved during the process.'

The renovation took several years, with Marloes and Bart undertaking almost all the work themselves and living in the property at the same time – an experience that wasn't without its challenges. 'I will never forget the storm during our first week,' Marloes says. 'The roof was leaking, so were the windows, and water was coming through the walls. We could shower but we had no heating, so we slept in front of the woodstove and woke to an inside temperature of only 8°C' – around 46°F.

The benefits of the couple's considered, hands-on approach are clear to see, however. They began by repairing the structure and installing much-needed radiators.

ROOM WITH A VIEW

Carved out of the formerly open-plan downstairs, the living area is a cosseting refuge whose wide picture window boasts a view extending one kilometre, over half a mile, into the distance (*this page*). 'Sometimes we cancel all weekend plans just to sit on the sofa, share a meal and watch the birds, the flowers and even visiting deer,' says Marloes. The other window faces the road and is dressed in semi-sheer linen drapes, giving privacy while letting in plenty of light.

CAREFULLY CONFIGURED

The living-area furniture has been arranged to aid the flow of light throughout the space. The bulkiest item – the sofa – is positioned away from the windows and paired with a round mirror (*opposite and above*). A steel-wire Diamond chair – a mid-century modern classic created by Italian-American designer Harry Bertoia in 1952 – makes a statement without obstructing light from any direction (*above right*).

However, the biggest alteration saw them build a new internal wall to divide the cavernous open-plan downstairs into a 'broken-plan' arrangement with distinct zones for relaxation, dining and cooking. It's a change that may sound counter-intuitive given the need to brighten the once-gloomy interior, but the series of smaller, defined spaces allows for a much cosier, more targeted lighting scheme. What's more, Marloes has maximized natural light at every opportunity through a clever use of colours, layout and materials.

Running throughout the house is a neutral palette that brings together pale beiges and off-whites, creating a calm, airy feel with a gentle underlying warmth. Richer tones in wooden pieces and accessories add depth without disrupting the soothing ambiance.

DINING ZONE

Branches and flowers collected on walks in the nearby woodland often take centre stage on the dining table (*this page*). This bespoke piece was made by Bijzondere Tafel, a Dutch furniture workshop that finds new uses for old timber.

MARLOES HAS MAXIMIZED NATURAL LIGHT AT EVERY OPPORTUNITY THROUGH A CLEVER USE OF COLOURS, LAYOUT AND MATERIALS

Meanwhile, furniture has been carefully positioned so as not to block the flow of light from one space to the next. After dark, floor and wall lamps, low-hanging pendants and candles in semi-translucent alabaster vessels create an inviting glow.

Also boosting the light are subtly reflective surfaces such as marble tabletops, patinated metal vases, mercury glass mirrors and polished concrete flooring. These are offset by tactile oak, linen and wool, resulting in layers of texture that take their cue from the great outdoors. 'Natural materials have such a timeless beauty,' says Marloes. 'They're especially important in a neutral interior, and I like to combine them in interesting ways – a jute rug on a concrete floor or a cane dining chair beneath a paper lamp.'

ON SHOW

Built-in shelving and a gnarled wooden plinth display treasured ceramics (*above left and above*). The artwork on the wall came from Dutch gallery Art-in-Return, which trades on an exchange basis rather than selling pieces for money. A large paper pendant casts a cosy glow over the dining table and provides a focal point that helps to define this area within the wider space (*opposite*).

A CONSIDERED KITCHEN

The kitchen evolved gradually as Marloes and Bart learned what they wanted from the space (*this page*). White unit fronts and a marble worktop bounce light from the window above the sink into the darker internal section, which has a Béton Ciré microcement counter. The upstand doubles as a display shelf for vases and accessories.

TEXTURAL APPEAL

A pair of stripped wooden doors encloses the kitchen larder, adding rustic texture that offsets the smoother surfaces (*this page*). Marloes originally bought them from a salvage sale for use in the couple's previous home and liked them so much that she brought them with her to repurpose when they moved. The wreath hanging from the handle was woven from hops grown by a neighbour.

Further textural contrasts appear in the walls, between bare plaster and crisp white paint. The ceilings, meanwhile, have been peeled back to the joists and whitewashed, enhancing the sense of light and space and adding another element of relaxed rusticity.

'The house gives us a deep feeling of comfort and it helps us to slow down,' explains Marloes. 'Every day I think how lucky we are to live here, and the fact that we did things almost entirely by ourselves makes it even more special. It may not have been our dream home from the beginning, but it's become one we never want to leave. It's part of us now, and we're part of it.'

SEATING NOOK

A small circular table, a built-in bench and classic Carl Hansen & Søn Wishbone chairs provide an informal breakfast and coffee spot in the corner of the kitchen (*this page and opposite*). The space is softened by a paper pendant lamp, linen cushions and snuggly sheepskins, with the latter becoming a favourite haunt of cats Josje and Bibi.

CRAFTED BY HAND

Marloes and Bart made the bathroom sink themselves, constructing a base from wood before covering it in Béton Ciré microcement with a water-resistant seal (*left*). The result merges almost seamlessly into the wall, making the compact space appear larger than it is. Stone floor tiles and a dark wooden stool reference the natural world, while a free-standing tub gives an air of quiet spa-like luxury (*above*).

RESTFUL RESTRAINT

The principal bedroom has been kept purposefully simple to aid rest and relaxation (*opposite*). Again, natural materials play a key role, with soft linen bedding alongside textured wooden bedside tables/nightstands. Elegant wall lamps provide versatile bedside lighting that can be angled wherever needed.

WOODLAND SANCTUARY

Hidden in protected woodland near the north Norfolk coast, Sarah Morton's beautiful cabin is clad in charred Accoya wood that almost blends into the surrounding trees. On the inside, however, it's a serene and airy retreat bathed in natural light. It's difficult to believe it was once a dilapidated garage covered in tatty yellow render.

Sarah, a former corporate lawyer, moved to Norfolk with her family in 2018. Both she and husband Daniel have fond memories of holidaying in the area as children – a tradition they continued after getting together and welcoming son George and daughter Charlotte, now 18 and 16. So, when they decided to swap the Hertfordshire commuter belt for a more relaxed life in the countryside, it was the obvious choice.

Their new home came with two acres of land and several outbuildings, plus multiple requests for visits from relatives and friends. Sarah and Daniel therefore set about converting the garage into guest accommodation with two bedrooms and a kitchenette. Work began in February 2020, but just two weeks later the UK Covid lockdown saw their builders down tools. This enforced interruption had a silver lining, though, allowing Sarah to rethink her ambitions for the space.

'I soon realized that to do justice to the building and its setting, we'd have to add more windows and commission custom joinery,' she explains. 'That meant increasing our budget, and so the idea of renovating it to become a business started to take shape. I was also looking for my next career move, and suddenly it all fell into place.'

LAID-BACK LOUNGING

The living room has windows on both sides, bringing in light throughout the day (*right*). 'I love sitting here in the early evening, looking out at the woodland and watching the golden-hour sunshine play on the walls and furniture,' says Sarah. A loose-cover linen sofa from Danish brand Tine K Home and a pair of safari-style chairs by French furniture maker Virginie Lobrot create an easy-going atmosphere.

MULTIFUNCTIONAL DESIGN

A microcement hearth extends from either side of the raised fireplace, providing a surface for lamps and ceramics (*above and above right*). One side is topped with a leather cushion and doubles as additional seating. The coffee table showcases the natural shape of the timber and was made bespoke by Yorkshire furniture workshop Galvin Brothers, who also crafted the fluted oak stools behind.

A PLACE TO GATHER

The bench seat in the dining area almost seems to grow out of the walls and is another nod to the adobe interiors that gave Sarah so much inspiration (*opposite*). She designed the table herself and commissioned Galvin Brothers to make it. Its trunk-like legs are echoed in the cylindrical rattan pendant lamps above.

A TACTILE KITCHEN

The beech kitchen cabinets are from British designer Sebastian Cox's range for deVOL (*left*). 'The tone and texture of the wood bring warmth into the space and contrast beautifully with the off-white walls,' Sarah says. 'I also like the detailing of the grooves and the patinated copper handles.'

ARTISAN FINDS

Many of the pieces in the cabin come from small businesses and independent makers, whom Sarah is keen to champion. Hand-crafted British hardwood chopping boards from Studio Arbor and a framed work by textile artist Charlotte Wakefield of Woven Form complete the kitchen scheme (*opposite*).

Sarah now rents the finished cabin out to paying guests as Blackwood Norfolk and has also developed a collection of hand-knotted rugs and cushions with homeware brand Lüks. But even though the space is run as a business, it's imbued with her personal, nature-inspired style.

'I have no formal training, but I've always had an interest in interior design and a flair for making things look nice,' she explains. 'I knew that I wanted the cabin to feel modern, uncluttered and relaxing, but without the coldness that I saw in many minimalist interiors. I started by putting together mood boards, and the images that really spoke to me had Southern Californian, Santa Fe and desert vibes. I was particularly drawn to houses in Joshua Tree' – a small town close to the national park of the same name – 'and the New Mexican adobe home of American artist Georgia O'Keeffe, so they were a big influence.'

The resulting scheme has a soft off-white base across the walls and ceilings, making the most of the shifting light provided by the cabin's dual east-west aspect. This is warmed by earthy beige, ochre and terracotta accents, as well as natural materials such as wood, clay, linen, wool and jute. It's a mix that Sarah describes as 'Scandifornian', and it suits the space perfectly.

The cabin is entered via a boot room with a fully glazed external door, a glass roof and a high clerestory window. Its tactile wooden cladding and built-in storage cupboards echo the solid beech cabinetry of the kitchen beyond, with the archway that connects the two spaces allowing natural light to flow between them.

JERUSALEM

CONNECTED SPACES

The kitchen units are referenced in the cladding and joinery of the boot room through the archway (*opposite*). It's the only part of the cabin that extends beyond the footprint of the original garage, providing handy storage and boosting natural light through its glazed door, roof light and clerestory window (*right*). Bowls by woodworker Alex Walshaw are displayed with ceramics and glassware in the kitchen (*below*).

The kitchen then opens up to a large living room, zoned into two through clever lighting and furniture placement. On one side is a cosy sitting area arranged around a contemporary microcement fireplace, with a long linen sofa, canvas easy chairs and a coffee table hewn from a single oak plank. On the other, Sarah has created a convivial dining space with built-in bench seating and a pair of rattan pendant lamps that spread soft, welcoming light over the table.

Two of the three bedrooms and their en-suite bathrooms are snuggled under the rafters on the floor above. Here, carefully positioned skylights illuminate beds, dressing tables, seating areas and basins, as well as lending a sense of spaciousness that counteracts the sloping ceilings. The largest of the bedrooms also features a floor-to-ceiling picture window for a wider panorama of the trees outside. Double-layered curtains and blackout blinds allow full control of the light and provide total darkness for sleeping.

'I love the connection with nature, and you really do appreciate that you're in the middle of the woods,' Sarah says. 'When I get the opportunity to be here on my own, it's deeply calming and relaxing, and that's exactly how I want my guests to feel, too.'

ABOVE IT ALL

As well as brightening the space, the skylights in the largest bedroom provide tantalizing glimpses of the treetops from the bed and sitting area (*opposite and below right*). The picture window has double curtains, with semi-sheer and thick linen layers that can be used to soften or shut out the light. Framed photography prints evoke the Californian landscapes that Sarah so loves.

DRESSING NOOK

The same bedroom has a floating dressing table with a hidden drawer and a tapered timber-stave stool (*below*). It's lit by a skylight above, with made-to-measure wardrobes/closets on either side maximizing storage beneath the sloping ceiling.

QUIET LUXURY

The basins in the en-suite bathrooms match the finish of the microcement walls and floors (*left*). This removes visual noise and blurs the boundaries between different elements, making the spaces seem calmer, brighter and airier. The shower enclosures are adorned with hanging plants, adding greenery to the neutral palette (*above*).

LOOKING UP

Tongue-and-groove panelling adds subtle texture to the smaller of the upstairs bedrooms, as well as drawing the eye upwards to the loftiest section of the space (*opposite*). The sense of height is aided by low-hanging pendant lamps from Melbourne-based studio IE Francis, which crafts lighting from sustainably sourced vegetable-tanned leather.

FOREST BATHING
**A timber-clad feature wall behind the egg-shaped tub in the downstairs bathroom speaks of the wooded landscape outside (*left*). The wood-block print on the shelf is by Block Shop Textiles and combines geometric forms with torn-edged cotton rag paper.
A rattan stool and a rustic clay vase of dried flowers soften the clean lines of the space (*opposite*).**

A SOFT OFF-WHITE BASE IS WARMED BY EARTHY ACCENTS, AS WELL AS NATURAL MATERIALS – IT'S A MIX THAT SARAH DESCRIBES AS 'SCANDIFORNIAN'

TOM
FORD

LAYOUT AND VIEW

Natural views provide a direct experience of nature, allowing us to observe not only the landscape but also changing seasons and weather patterns. I mentioned earlier in this book that people recover faster from surgery when they can gaze over vegetation or water, and this visual connection with nature contributes to our daily wellbeing, too. Even the tiniest glimpse of treetops or the sky can have a positive impact, revealing the shifting leaves, the wind rustling in the branches and the clouds flitting overhead.

The way we lay out our homes helps us to make the most of whatever view we have, and it's also an opportunity to evoke the natural world through spatial planning. Furniture placement and room configurations can be used to replicate the environments that have allowed us humans to live and thrive for hundreds of thousands of years – environments that we're genetically programmed to find appealing. It requires a bit of thought and experimentation, but the end result is a home that works better on aesthetic, functional and psychological levels.

NATURAL VIEWS

If you're lucky enough to have any view of nature, whether it be sweeping countryside, an urban park or your own garden, look at ways to enhance it. Position seating, tables and beds where you can admire the vista, and don't block it with bulky items or heavy window dressings (*opposite*). You could also use mirrors to make it visible from additional corners, frame it by placing pieces on either side or highlight it by angling furniture to form a clear visual pathway towards it.

If you have no natural view, you can create one with potted plants or a window box, or simulate one by hanging or propping a picture of a landscape on your wall (*above*). They sound like small measures, but research has shown that simply looking at an image of nature can reduce stress, fatigue and blood pressure, and improve our overall mood.

PROSPECT AND REFUGE

We're hardwired to feel most comfortable in settings that offer both protection and a view outwards. It's known as prospect-refuge theory and it's another legacy of our hunter-gatherer past, when our survival depended on hiding from predators in caves and forests while scanning the landscape for threats and opportunities. Few of us these days face the same challenges as our ancestors, but we're still instinctively drawn towards partially enclosed spaces that retain a visual connection with our surroundings. If given the choice in a restaurant, for instance, most of us would opt for a table around the edge where we can observe other diners rather than taking centre stage ourselves.

Prospect-refuge theory can be applied in the home through easy measures such as adding a window seat or creating a cosy reading nook in an alcove or niche that faces the wider space (*left*). Even installing booth-like banquettes around a dining table and swapping regular chairs for wraparound designs can provide the sense of shelter we crave. We can use prospect-refuge theory to improve our sleeping arrangements, too, forming cocooning nests with high headboards, and giving children cabin beds or canopies to help them feel snug and secure.

ZONING AND BROKEN-PLAN ARRANGEMENTS

Open-plan living has become very popular, but prospect-refuge theory holds that spaces that are too open can make us feel anxious and exposed. Broken-plan layouts, which are divided into distinct zones while maintaining a sense of flow, are much better suited to our evolutionary make-up.

You can break up open spaces with partial walls and changes in floor level (*right*), or with less permanent means such as shelving units, screens, curtains and plants (*far right*). You can also define different zones with rugs and lighting (perhaps a large pendant lamp over a table or sitting area), and by grouping furniture into inviting clusters. Conversely, if a fully enclosed room feels confining, consider installing internal glazing or swapping conventional doors for pocket designs that slide back into the walls.

MYSTERY AND ENTICEMENT

As well as seeking prospect and refuge, we have an innate desire to explore. Biophilic design taps into this by using layout to pique our curiosity and tempt us to venture further into a space.

Think about creating sightlines within your home, drawing the eye with strategically placed pieces that offer an intriguing hint of what lies beyond. When looking through a doorway, for example, a large plant or a statement chair is much more enticing than a blank wall or the side of a wardrobe/armoire (*above*). Also make sure there are clear routes through each space and on to the next, and put the same effort into designing hallways, corridors and landings as you would any other room. All too often an afterthought, these transitional spaces serve as connections between different areas and should be aesthetically pleasing, practical and easy to navigate. A tidy hallway with a beautifully styled console table creates a welcoming first impression that makes you want to see more; tripping over coats as you squeeze past a cumbersome cabinet does not.

ASYMMETRICAL BALANCE

I've touched on symmetry and asymmetry in relation to shape and pattern, but they come into play with room layout, too. As a species we're drawn towards symmetry, but natural landscapes are never fully symmetrical and so mirror-image arrangements, where each side of a space matches the other perfectly, can seem stiff and contrived.

Asymmetrical balance provides a neat solution. It involves using items that carry a similar visual weight but aren't identical – a tall cupboard opposite a large artwork, or a floor lamp at one end of a sofa and a side table topped with a table lamp at the other. This creates a sense of equilibrium with enough variety to keep things interesting, resulting in a home that feels effortless and natural (*below*).

GARDEN CONNECTION

When Merrett Houmøller Architects and Stephen Nash of interior-design studio All & Nxthing joined forces to transform a Victorian terrace in north London, the result was a tranquil city sanctuary that blurs the boundaries between indoors and out.

A RADICAL RECONFIGURATION

Emily and Stephen opted for a dramatic double-height extension for the kitchen and dining area (*above and opposite*). 'It meant losing a bedroom, but it was worth it for the openness, light and sense of volume,' explains Stephen. 'This is without question the heart of our home. It's where we can gather or just be together and doing our own thing. One of us might be reading in the corner while another cooks and our son plays nearby.'

It's something their client Emily had long desired. 'The idea of bringing nature inside has resonated with me since childhood,' she says. 'I remember the forest entering Max's bedroom in the book *Where the Wild Things Are*, and that kind of magical realism has always appealed to me. It's certainly shaped what I wanted in a home.'

Luckily, she and her husband, also called Stephen, found just the property for turning the dream into a reality. 'We were immediately struck by the house's potential,' Stephen recalls. 'It was likely built around 1896, and it's larger than many others in the area. What truly made it stand out, though, was the setting. It backs onto a patch of woodland, which gives it privacy and a connection to nature while still being right in London. That combination – greenery, quietness, a sense of retreat – was incredibly compelling.'

The couple's brief to the designers was a home that's open, minimalist and filled with light, but also warm and inviting – a space for gathering with friends, as well as enjoying time with their young son and Stephen's grown-up children. They also wanted to reference places they've travelled to and loved. 'I've spent a lot of time in Morocco and the Middle East, and we're both drawn to the textures and tones of the Mediterranean,' Emily explains. 'Having recently lived in California, I was also inspired by its indoor-outdoor lifestyle and desert-modern aesthetic. We wanted the house to feel grounded, natural and, above all, calm.'

Taking their cue from Moroccan riads and traditional Andalusian homes, which often consist of multiple rooms arranged around a tall central courtyard, Merrett Houmøller Architects added a double-height rear extension with soaring trapezoidal ceilings. This is connected to the original section of the house by internal openings and sloping piers, creating a series of interlocking spaces – some airy and expansive; others cosy and secluded.

INSIDE OUT

The extension's brick floor flows into the garden, creating a seamless transition between indoors and out (*above*). A long oak table, leather chairs and a vase of dried grasses bring further natural texture to the dining area, which is zoned by sloping walls and ceilings that add a sense of cosiness to the tall, open-plan space.

ROUGH WITH SMOOTH

Natural materials ground the kitchen within the lofty extension. Most of the walls are lined with clay plaster, whose warm tones are carried through into the sawn maple-wood units and patinated copper worktops. However, one section has been left bare to showcase the brickwork (*above and opposite*). 'It's a nice reminder of the original fabric of the building,' says Stephen Nash.

THE COUPLE'S BRIEF TO THE DESIGNERS WAS A HOME THAT'S OPEN, MINIMALIST AND FILLED WITH LIGHT, BUT ALSO WARM AND INVITING

THE LEBANESE COOKBOOK
OTTOLENGHI SIMPLE

Angular windows frame views of the garden and the trees beyond that are visible throughout the downstairs, while high-level glazing brings light deep into the building.

Echoes of Morocco and the Mediterranean are also present in the colour and material choices. 'The interior design incorporates raw, natural textures such as exposed brick, unfired clay and limewash-painted walls,' explains Stephen Nash from All & Nxthing. 'These are complemented by bespoke band-sawn joinery, oxidized copper kitchen work surfaces and unlacquered brass fittings. The materials were selected for their ability to patinate over time, giving warmth, tactility and a sense of continuity throughout the space.'

GOING UP

The staircase has been updated with sleek steel banisters topped by a gently curved oak rail (*below left*). It emerges onto a balcony-like landing overlooking the kitchen and dining area below, again evoking the internal courtyards that are common in Morocco and Spain (*opposite*).

WATERSIDE LIVING

The angles of the architecture are echoed in a long cushioned bench, which was designed to be both sculptural and functional (*below*). One end has a planter integrated into the seat and overlooks a shallow rain-fed pool that casts dancing reflections across the walls and ceilings. 'On sunny days, we love watching the light play off the water,' says Emily.

DOUBLE DUTY

The middle section of the downstairs is a multifunctional space for relaxing and home working (*opposite and this page*). Although it has no window of its own, light streams in through internal openings that also provide views of the garden. The custom-made cabinetry has angular cupboards that reference the trapezoidal forms of the extension, while an asymmetric Sideways sofa by Danish designer Rikke Frost for Carl Hansen & Søn adds contrasting organic curves.

COHESIVE THREADS
With its Victorian bay window and white-painted walls, the living room has a relaxed yet refined feel (*this page*). There are nods to the extension in the warm tones of the rug and furniture, the large potted plants and the triangular shapes of the travertine coffee table, ensuring a sense of harmony throughout the house.

JENNY ROSE-INNES
TIDE
THESIGER CROSSING THE SANDS
S Giles Sparrow

SIMPLE SOPHISTICATION

The principal bedroom is understated, uncluttered and bright (*left and right*). There is subtle warmth and tactility in the pink velvet daybed, stone fireplace, linen curtains, fabric pendant lamp and patterned rug, all of which hint at the colours and materials used downstairs. Fitted wardrobes/closets provide plenty of storage.

It's a palette that serves to further strengthen the link between inside and out, too. The brick floor, for example, extends into the garden, creating an unbroken visual and physical connection. This is reinforced by lots of indoor greenery, with planters incorporated into built-in bench seating and half-height dividing walls.

The living room at the front of the house largely retains its original footprint, as does the principal bedroom located on the floor above. Both spaces are painted in a simple off-white shade, but they also maintain a relationship with the extension through salmon-pink accents, wooden cabinetry and leafy plants.

The peach-toned tadelakt finish of the family bathroom, meanwhile, is another homage to Moroccan architecture.

'We wanted to take the things that have inspired Emily and Stephen and guide them into a cohesive design, with natural materials, textures and spatial qualities creating a home that's personal and deeply restful,' says Stephen Nash.

They've achieved just that. 'The finished house is uncluttered yet warm, open yet intimate,' adds Emily. 'It's a refuge – somewhere to retreat at the end of the day – but it's also a welcoming space that brings people together. And it's encouraging us to slow down – to find joy in less rather than constantly seeking more.'

JUST PEACHY

The bathroom is covered in peach-coloured tadelakt, a lime- based Moroccan plaster that combines visual depth with a smooth, waterproof finish (*above and right*). The curvaceous sink unit appears to grow organically from the wall, and the shower enclosure features a hidden planter with cascading greenery. Brass fittings and a solid limestone floor add further warmth to the space.

A VIEW FROM ABOVE

Despite living on the eighth floor of an urban apartment block, artist Savita Hartsteen has long drawn inspiration from nature. Her Rotterdam home in the Netherlands, which she shares with her IT-consultant husband Ramon and Golden Retriever Indie, is a peaceful sanctuary decorated in natural tones and textures. And, with its sweeping view, considered layout and cosy corners, it's a wonderful example of biophilic zoning and prospect-refuge theory in action.

It was the view, in fact, that first drew the couple to the property. 'The kitchen and living area have large floor-to-ceiling windows that create an airy atmosphere and fill the apartment with light,' says Savita. 'And we just love the expansive, unobstructed vista. Even though we're in a busy city, being up high and looking out over the buildings, streets and squares below brings a deep sense of tranquillity.'

Savita and Ramon moved into the apartment in 2010 and, with limited funds, made a few minor tweaks to the decor. Over the years their budget grew, as did their understanding of exactly what they needed from their home, and so a more comprehensive renovation followed in 2020. 'Both of us are quite sensitive by nature, and I in particular can easily feel overwhelmed by the fast pace of city life,' Savita explains. 'Having a home that feels like a true retreat became essential – not just aesthetically, but also for our wellbeing.'

Savita's vision was a serene, softly minimalist and meaningful space that takes its cue from the natural settings where she feels happiest. 'Every morning I take a 15-minute drive out of the city with Indie to find some stillness among the open landscape of a nearby nature reserve. It's a big inspiration for me, and more than just a visual one. Nature isn't only something you see, it's something you experience, and I wanted my home to reflect the way this precious time outdoors makes me feel.'

RELAXED DINING

Savita describes the dining area as 'an island within the wider space' (*above left and opposite*). The circular oak table and curvaceous Beetle chairs (a contemporary classic from Danish brand GUBI) invite slow meals and convivial evenings with family and friends. A Formakami rice-paper pendant lamp by Spanish designer Jaime Hayon for &Tradition is a focal point overhead. The windows have pull-down blinds/shades, allowing the couple to feel as connected or removed from the city as they want.

INNER SANCTUARY

The living area is furthest from the windows and has two sofas angled towards each other (*this page*). It is a semi-enclosed refuge that still benefits from a view outwards. The sofas' clean-lined, boxy shapes are offset by rounded lamps and tables, as well as by the flowing forms of the artwork on the wall behind.

THE KINFOLK HOME
Minimalista
NORDIC MOODS
SKANDINAVISCH WOHNEN Sarah von Heugel
STILL

The layout of the apartment is a key part of this. Within the main living space, Savita has created three distinct zones, each with its own purpose and focal point – and each positioned to benefit from the view. The kitchen is centred around an island unit, providing a sociable place to cook or linger while gazing out over Rotterdam. Beyond this, a circular table beneath a large pendant lamp creates an intimate and welcoming dining area. The two sofas, meanwhile, sit perpendicularly to each other in the innermost section, forming a refuge where the couple can withdraw without losing sight of the windows.

A neutral palette of beiges, greys and soft whites runs across the various zones, ensuring the overall scheme is unified rather than disjointed. It's a selection that was itself inspired by the natural world, as Savita explains: 'These hues remind me of sand, stone and other elements that I love. Just like in nature, where colours blend effortlessly to create a harmonious whole, they make the apartment feel balanced and soothing.' The result is a space with an easy sense of flow, with large artworks (most of them Savita's own), sideboard/credenza displays and gallery walls that invite the eye to wander from one area to the next.

When it comes to materials, Savita is drawn to the tactile and the organic. 'To add layers of texture, I use soft cushions and throws, ribbed rice-paper lamps that create a gentle, diffused light and ceramic vases that introduce subtle earthy elements. Our oak flooring brings warmth underfoot, and I like to incorporate wooden details in other spots, too. Marble appears in small accents, such as the bases of lamps and tables.'

Savita concludes: 'Ramon and I dream of one day living in a rural house surrounded by trees, but that's not our reality yet. So for now, I have created an interior that carries the calm feeling of nature into the city. This apartment is our safe haven – a place where we can slow down, unwind and recharge. No matter what the day has been like, coming home always brings a sense of peace and comfort.'

WITHIN THE MAIN LIVING SPACE, SAVITA HAS CREATED THREE DISTINCT ZONES, EACH WITH ITS OWN PURPOSE AND FOCAL POINT

PERSONAL TOUCHES

The sideboard/credenza along the living-area wall provides a place to display favourite ceramics and other objects, including a vase in the shape of a shell and an abstract interpretation of a bird (*opposite*). Dimmable lamps and flickering candles allow Savita and Ramon to change the mood from bright and energizing to cosy and relaxing (*above*).

WINDOW SEAT

The apartment has deep windowsills, one of which Savita has turned into a cosy corner where she can settle back and watch the world go by (*this page*). 'I love sitting here in the evening, reflecting on my day as the sun goes down and the city lights slowly appear.'

ISLAND LIFE

Indie relaxes in the kitchen by the large island unit, which maximizes surface and storage space while also making the most of the view (*this page*). 'We made sure the bar stools face the windows,' Savita says. 'Now, I start my day here with a cup of coffee, looking out and enjoying the moment.'

ORGANIC ELEMENTS

Artworks and ceramics add shape and texture to the minimalist white kitchen (*left and opposite*). Hanging on the wall is one of Savita's own paintings, which combine natural pigments with materials such as sand. 'My work explores quiet transformations, and the parallels between the natural world and our experiences – how everything is constantly shifting, changing and leaving traces over time,' she explains.

KRUPS

FORAGED FINDS

Savita likes to bring home flowers and foliage from her daily walks in nature (*above*). 'They're small reminders of how happy and grounded they make me feel,' she says. In the corner of the bedroom, for example, a sculptural magnolia branch is on display alongside an irregular, puddle-shaped mirror and a tall, wavy candlestick – themselves subtle references to the natural world.

LAYERED UP

Appealing layers of texture add depth to the calming beige decor of the bedroom (*this page*). The bed is dressed in soft linen sheets and a woollen throw, while the bedside tables/nightstands are adorned with marble-based Kizu lamps from New Works. Suspended overhead is a simple rice-paper pendant, and on the wall behind is another of Savita's textural artworks.

BRITISH DESIGNERS AT HOME
JENNY ROSE-INNES
HIGH TIDE
WILFRED THESIGER CROSSING THE SANDS
COSMOS
Giles Sparrow

FINISHING TOUCHES

When it comes to interiors, small details can have a big impact. The objects that you choose to display add interest and character. They're the icing on the design cake that brings everything else together, enhancing the overall scheme and making a space feel lived in and loved.

We've already explored how art and accessories can introduce natural colours, materials, shapes, patterns and motifs or create a view of nature where there is none. But these finishing touches tie into biophilic design in other ways, too. Plants and flowers bring nature into a space; other items can be used to emulate it through considered styling and beautifully composed vignettes. They also offer a means to conjure up the aromas of the natural world and appeal to our most emotive sense, scent.

Whether you rent or own, these are the things that make a home truly yours, contributing to that all-important sense of belonging and rootedness that I discussed earlier (see page 49).

PLANTS

I began this book by stating that biophilic design is about much more than plants, but they do have an important role to play (*opposite*). As well as contributing to our general health and wellbeing (think of those post-surgery hospital patients once again), they release oxygen and moisture into the air, lessening the fatigue, dry eyes and headaches caused by stale indoor environments. They can even improve acoustics by absorbing sound – handy if you live near a busy road.

The many benefits of plants mean that indoor gardens and living walls are becoming increasingly popular in commercial and healthcare settings. Few of us have the space or budget to install them in the home, but you can create a similar effect by clustering plants together, positioning them at different heights around a room or cascading them down from shelves, hanging planters and plant stands (*above*).

Always choose varieties that are suited to the light conditions and humidity levels of the space and the amount of care you're able to provide. There are hardy options that will survive even the gloomiest of corners or most neglectful of owners, and a good plant shop will be able to advise.

FLOWERS, FOLIAGE AND FORAGED FINDS

Flowers and foliage are an easy way to bring nature into a space, and you needn't splash out on expensive bouquets. A single stem drooping gracefully from a vase can be just as beautiful as an elaborate arrangement, as can a simple bunch of dried grasses or a wild branch picked up on a walk (*above*). Other natural treasures include pebbles, pinecones and shells, which can be displayed in bowls or dotted artfully along shelves. Larger rocks and sections of driftwood, meanwhile, make stunning sculptures on coffee tables, sideboards and plinths.

If you're foraging, always do so responsibly. Never take anything from private land without permission, or damage plants and trees by disturbing their roots or snipping off large sections. Removing material from beaches can worsen coastal erosion and is in fact illegal in the UK and some other countries. Finally, check what you're gathering – harmless cow parsley/Queen Anne's lace, for example, bears a close resemblance to deadly poison hemlock!

CELEBRATING THE SEASONS

In centuries past, almost every aspect of human life was governed by the seasons. Nowadays, our fast-paced, indoor lifestyles mean it's all too easy to switch off from the cyclical changes taking place beyond our windows, but reattuning ourselves to these rhythms can foster a deep connection with nature, encouraging us to slow down and appreciate the moment.

Each season brings its own beauty: blossom and blooms in spring and summer, berries and vibrant foliage in autumn, bare branches and evergreen boughs in winter. You can celebrate them with floral displays, wreaths and garlands, and with seasonal produce arranged in bowls or on sideboards and mantelpieces (*below*). You can even channel the changing seasons through the textures, colours and materials you use in your home, building up a collection of different cushions, throws and accessories to swap in and out according to the time of year – perhaps lighter tones and breezy linen in spring and summer, richer hues and snuggly wool in autumn and winter.

SCENT

Scent is a powerful tool for evoking nature. It's processed by our olfactory bulb, which is directly linked to the areas of the brain associated with emotion, and the slightest trace can trigger a memory or feeling. There are many ways to incorporate natural fragrances in the home, including scented candles, essential oils, reed diffusers, room sprays, herb bundles, potpourri and scented garlands (*above*). They provide yet another way to mark the changing seasons, and you can also use them to alter the mood of a space in line with your circadian rhythm – perhaps with a zingy citrus aroma in the morning and calming lavender come evening.

STYLING TIPS AND TRICKS

As we've already established, natural landscapes aren't uniform or one-dimensional; they contain layers of interest and depth, with varied shapes and sizes. You can reflect this in the way you style accessories on shelves and other surfaces (*above*). Rather than spacing things evenly, group them together into vignettes, with smaller items overlapping larger ones. Odd numbers generally appear more natural to the eye than even ones, so try interspersing single objects with clusters of three and five. Place some things on books or trays to add height if everything looks a bit flat. And if you're struggling, choose one favourite piece as a starting point and go from there.

CURATED CALM

'Detail-oriented minimalism' is how interior designer Holly Marder sums up the Dutch home in Rotterdam that she and her team created for client Margreet van Staalduijnen. It's a fitting description, as the house demonstrates how every aspect of decoration, from instantly noticeable elements such as colour and material choices right down to the smallest finishing touches, can be used to foster a deep connection with the natural world.

Margreet and her partner purchased the four-storey property off-plan in 2019 and enlisted Holly, founder of Avenue Design Studio in nearby The Hague, in the early stages of construction. Their aim: to mould the inside into a welcoming city sanctuary for themselves and their young children, inspired in part by Nordic minimalism and in part by the craftsmanship and understated aesthetics they had encountered on a recent trip to Japan.

'From the outset, our vision was to create a family home that honours the contemporary architectural character of the house while reflecting Margreet's appreciation for sophisticated simplicity and tactility,' Holly explains. 'We wanted to design spaces that feel quietly luxurious – spaces with clean lines and thoughtful detailing, where form and function exist in perfect balance.'

The house has a somewhat unusual layout, with the kitchen opening up to a double-height dining area backed by a dramatic wall of glass. Stairs lead from here up to a mezzanine living room, with an enclosed study behind. The bedrooms then occupy the top two floors and have large picture windows overlooking a square of gardens at the rear.

Holly's priority was to celebrate the ample natural light that this arrangement brings and improve the spatial flow. She therefore commissioned room dividers inspired by traditional Japanese *koushi-do* (latticework doors).

CALL OF THE WILD

In the dining area, abstract representations of nature are present in the stoneware bowls, crafted by Belgian ceramicist Patrice Lesueur of Lava Collective and reminiscent of seedheads and tree bark (*above left*). The silk and linen wall hanging was commissioned from Mallorca-based textile artist Adriana Meunié and depicts a Japanese heron (*opposite*). The table is by Japanese company Karimoku New Standard, and the chairs are Hans J. Wegner's classic CH23 design for Carl Hansen & Søn.

SOPHISTICATED CONTRASTS

Made by KOAK Design, the kitchen offsets dark-stained bamboo with pale stone and opal-glass pendant lamps (*this page*). The grid-like pattern of the cabinets echoes the sliding Japanese-style latticework doors, which separate the space from the entrance hall at the front of the house.

ALL IN THE DETAIL

The kitchen storage includes large areas of open shelving, where glasses and tableware sit on display (*opposite and above*). These include hand-carved wooden bowls and clay pieces with mottled glazes that resemble rock and stone. At one end of the work surface, a bundle of dried herbs rests in a raised display bowl (*above right*).

Their sliding construction offers maximum flexibility, allowing spaces to be opened up or closed off as needed, with the vertical slats giving privacy yet enabling light to filter from one area to the next. The same slatted design appears on a pair of screens atop the balustrade in the living room, where it lends a cosy sense of refuge – and keeps active little ones safe – without blocking any light.

For the colour palette, Holly and her team opted for muted tones that enhance the sense of space and tranquillity. 'Subtle neutrals, gentle greys and rich, earthy hues create depth and contrast, highlighting statement elements such as bespoke furniture, artworks, large lantern-like pendant lamps and vintage pieces,' she says. The materials were also chosen with serenity in mind. 'To soften the hard, modern feel of the newly built house, we incorporated warm wood and bamboo in varying tones, along with natural stone and textiles.'

Thoughtful styling adds soul to this restful backdrop. Many of the decorative accessories were sourced via A. Gallery, which Holly runs alongside her design studio to showcase handmade works by independent artists, artisans and makers. Among them are vases, ceramics and other objects with flowing forms and tactile materials, often displayed in clusters or arranged into carefully composed vignettes. The marble coffee

STILL

BALCONY SEAT

A bouclé sofa, vintage art, chocolate marble coffee tables and slatted screens add balance and cosiness to the mezzanine living room, which overlooks the dining area below (*this page*). The 1930s oak chair is the work of French furniture maker Charles Dudouyt, known for his focus on natural materials and unusual decorative details such as the wooden spheres on the armrests.

SHELF LIFE

At the rear of the living room, off-centre bamboo shelving provides a home for ceramics and natural objects such as a large chunk of rose quartz (*top left, far above left and opposite*). There are also built-in marble-topped storage cupboards where less aesthetically pleasing items can be hidden from view – essential in a busy family home (*above left*).

LAYERS OF DETAIL, NEUTRAL COLOURS, NATURAL MATERIALS AND AN ABUNDANCE OF LIGHT MAKE FOR A HARMONIOUS URBAN OASIS

KARIN SLAUGHTER
PIEP ZEI DE MUIS
MARC LAMMERS
DE BEURS OP LIJN VIER

STUDY SPACE

The study is accessed through another pair of sliding doors, their slats backed by glass to enable peaceful home working even when the adjoining living room is in use (*opposite*). Practicality was the key consideration here, but there are nevertheless natural references in the choice of materials and in small items such as beeswax candles with irregular, tree-trunk-like forms.

SCULPTURAL ADDITIONS

Statement vases with organic shapes are dotted around Margreet's home, providing a link with the natural world even when empty of flowers and foliage (*above and above right*). On the circular table at one end of the study is a large vessel with drip glazing in shades of green and gold, handmade by A. Gallery's resident ceramicist C. van der Meeren. The chairs are from sustainable Danish furniture studio TAKT.

tables in the living room, for example, are dressed with a trio of textured clay vases in differing heights; on the shelving unit at the far end of the space, smaller items are placed in front of larger ones, generating visual interest that mimics the depth and complexity of the natural world. There are also paintings, drawings and wall hangings depicting flora, fauna and wooded landscapes.

These layers of detail, combined with neutral colours, natural materials and an abundance of light, make for a harmonious urban oasis that's pared-back yet brimming with character. 'Everything works together to form a home that feels effortless yet curated, timeless yet modern,' says Holly. 'With aspects drawn from Scandinavian interior styles, Japanese tradition and nature, it's a perfect reflection of our clients and their needs.'

SOAK AND SLEEP

The principal bedroom is a simple, soothing space with an in-room bathtub set in the innermost corner (*this page and opposite*). The wall behind the bed is adorned with a monochrome landscape drawing and a textural sculpture made from mulberry bark and asparagus peel by Dutch paper artist Loes Schepens, who wanted to emulate the tree bark found on forest walks. Natural materials are also present in a linen bedspread, a jute bathmat, a wooden stool and a bedside table/nightstand made from blackened, roughly hewn oak.

PLAYFUL TOUCHES

House-shaped bunk beds provide cocooning sleep spaces in the children's rooms, one of which also features a swing (*opposite and this page*). This is a fun addition that appears in many biophilic spaces thanks to the rhythmic swaying motion, which emulates movement in nature and is known to ease anxiety.

SEASONAL STYLE

Nature and its shifting seasons have influenced much of the Lincolnshire home of Jade Jordan-James, founder of interior styling and creative consultancy Wild in the Wolds, and her husband Rob, a civil engineer. In fact the outside world is evident in almost every aspect, from the colours on the walls to the pretty displays of flowers and foliage dotted here and there.

The couple hadn't been planning to relocate from their previous base on England's south coast, but stumbled across an online listing for an 1820s villa in the market town of Louth during the 2020 Covid lockdown. 'We'd always dreamed of owning a double-fronted Georgian home like this, and we couldn't stop thinking about it,' Jade recalls. 'We went to view it in person as soon as restrictions were lifted, and we fell in love with it the moment we stepped inside. It's full of beautiful period features but it also has a calm presence, and we could immediately envision making it our own.'

The house needed a lot of care, however. Originally built by a corn and wool merchant, it has had many incarnations, having been converted into flats in the 1960s and then back into a single dwelling in the 1990s. 'One former owner even used it to rear pigs, and in an uncanny coincidence his son is now our postman!' says Jade with a laugh.

No signs of this stint as a pigsty remain, with Jade and Rob having replaced pipework and wiring, replastered and repainted, reinstated missing ceiling roses and cornicing/molding and installed two new bathrooms.

NATURAL ELEGANCE

The living room was the first space that Jade and Rob renovated and it set the tone for the rest of the house (*right*). Its soft beige walls are offset by an inky blue-grey velvet sofa, while natural materials are introduced through antique wooden furniture, a marble-topped coffee table and a large earthenware vase.